A FAMILY OBSESSION

What We Talk About When We Talk About Football

Harry & Jamie Redknapp
with Leo Moynihan

CONSTABLE

CONSTABLE

First published in Great Britain in 2024 by Constable
This paperback edition published in 2025 by Constable

1 3 5 7 9 10 8 6 4 2

All photographs from authors' collection unless otherwise specified.

A CIP catalogue record for this book
is available from the British Library.

ISBN: 978-1-40872-174-2

Typeset in Adobe Caslon Pro by SX Composing DTP, Rayleigh, Essex
Printed and bound in Great Britain by Clays Ltd, Elcograf S.p.A.

Papers used by Constable are from well-managed forests
and other responsible sources.

Constable
An imprint of
Little, Brown Book Group
Carmelite House
50 Victoria Embankment
London EC4Y 0DZ

The authorised representative
in the EEA is
Hachette Ireland
8 Castlecourt Centre, Dublin 15,
D15 XTP3, Ireland
(email: info@hbgi.ie)

An Hachette UK Company
www.hachette.co.uk

www.littlebrown.co.uk

HARRY REDKNAPP was born in 1947 in East London. After starting out as a trainee at Tottenham, he signed for West Ham and played for them between 1965 and 1972. He also played for Bournemouth and the Seattle Sounders before injury took him into management and coaching. He has managed at Bournemouth, West Ham, Portsmouth (twice), Southampton, Tottenham Hotspur, QPR and has had stints at Birmingham and the Jordan national team. He won the FA Cup with Portsmouth in 2008 and took Spurs into the Champions League in 2010. He is married to Sandra and has two sons, Mark and Jamie.

Born in Hampshire in 1973, JAMIE REDKNAPP made his debut for Bournemouth at the age of sixteen. He signed for Liverpool in 1991 and stayed at Anfield until 2002, in the process making more than three hundred appearances, scoring in excess of forty goals and winning the League Cup in 1995. Redknapp subsequently played for Tottenham Hotspur and Southampton, and won seventeen caps for England. He retired in 2005. Jamie is a principal pundit on Sky Sports' football coverage and is a team captain on Sky's two-time BAFTA-winning sports panel show *A League of Their Own*. He has three children and lives in London.

We'd both like to dedicate this book to our beautiful wives,
Sandra and Frida. Thank you for everything you do.
To all our family for their never-ending support
and to Jamie's boys, Charley, Beau and Rapha.
Keep the passion alive.

Contents

Falling in love . . .

JAMIE

It's just the two of us. We're sat in an empty dressing room, not long after a match. It's been one of the decent ones. A long slog from the south coast to a far northern town, and in front of a little over a thousand people, we've worked hard and fought for our draw. The smells of football fill our nostrils. Liniment oil, Deep Heat, shower gel and old aftershave. Sock ties and gaffer tape lie on the floor, and droplets of condensation from the hot showers slowly make their way down the walls.

Dad has that wry grin on his face. Not the big beamer he would be wearing had we won, but it's been a good day. Hard work, organisation, good football, all the things he loves about managing in the game.

He's happy with me. I'm seventeen, I've been doing OK, training well, grafting, listening, mixing it with senior pros, learning the trade that I've always wanted to perfect and make mine. Today, I've played well. Today, I stood out.

Things were coming off for me. I was playing the way I wanted to play. Everything me and my dad have ever talked about was there.

Effort. That's always a given.

Availability. I'm showing for my teammates, wanting it to feet, give, go and get it back.

Passing. My head is up. I'm looking after possession, play it easy, and again, be patient, waiting for the killer ball. Making things happen.

Bravery. I'm getting kicked. My opponent in a Third Division midfield is no choirboy, and he hasn't held back. He's out to make my life difficult, to intimidate me, to let me know this ain't no picnic. I'm not moaning, though. I have no problem with all of that or with him. I play the game. That's what I've learned, that's what Dad has drilled into me. Take the kicks, take the knocks, ride the challenges, run off the pain.

I love it. It feels right. I hate the final whistle. It's been a good day.

Now, it's just Dad and me. I have chosen to play lower league football for a reason. I want to be here among it. I've chosen to travel the country every week. To play, not to watch. I have turned down a big First Division club. Their facilities, their superstars, all very nice, but I want to be here, surrounded by the real game. I want to take the knocks, hear the jokes, be a footballer. A proper footballer. Study and get better. Dad has that smile on his face. Maybe that's what I'm doing. Getting better.

Now, though, another top-flight club have shown an interest in me – the biggest club and they are managed by the biggest name. He has courted me, invited me up, he's phoned my dad fifty times, but no decision has been made. Not yet. Doubts have crept in. Still a lot to learn? Is it too soon?

We stand in the dressing room, alone. It's quiet. Dad is still smiling.

'You all right, H?' I ask.

'Yeah, I'm good, son,' he says.

'What is it?'

There's a pause.

'You're ready.'

If I was ready, a lot of that was down to my dad, my family and a lifelong passion for football that over three decades later shows no sign of decreasing. At the heart of all of that is my dad. Harry Redknapp, football manager and king of the *I'm a Celebrity* jungle to most, but to me he's a dad who I have followed around football pitches and stadiums since I could walk. With each step, he helped to harbour a love for the game that has been such a big part of our family's life.

Dad got it from his dad, a keen footballer and obsessive watcher of the game. Dad passed it to me and my brother, Mark, and now, as all three of us stand side by side on some damp touchline somewhere in the south of the country, watching one of our boys grow and play the game, I can stand there and can't help but celebrate how much football, like some old lifelong pet in the corner of the family living room, is always with us, somehow binding us all together.

We're a pretty normal bunch. A family. A doting mum, a loving dad, grandkids, in-laws, laughs and tears. Marriages, births, funerals and get-togethers. We move around, we live apart, but somehow we are always together. A firm bond.

A big part of that glue is football. We are not alone. We are no different to families all over the country and the world. The game has that strength. As a teenager with teenage outlooks on life, I would sit with my grandad – Pops we called him. An old docker, he lived through the war, saw things that I, as a young kid growing up near the New Forest, never would. I could listen to him all day, but what he liked to talk about most was football. That'll do me. We sadly lost Pops, but we, like so many families, will never lose football.

There are the matches we have seen together, or seen apart but have come back to with a phone call. 'Did you see the game?' As regular a start to a conversation as hello. There are the players. I will never tire of asking Dad about the greats he watched and played against. Drilling at his coalface of knowledge, demanding memories of a George Best shimmy or laughing at how the great Bobby Moore would iron his socks. Insight after insight. Memory upon memory.

Players, managers, tournaments, controversies and moments of magic. Family debates and disagreements. Who is the greatest and why? What team of old would have beaten the great teams of today? They never end and they never will, and then one day, I will be telling my grandkids about the players I saw and marvelled at from both out on the pitch and in the stands.

Our story is a little different to most in as much as Dad and I both played the game and, in a strange twist of fate, I started and ended my career calling him 'boss'. Don't tell him this, but maybe he always has been.

Today, I am fascinated by what makes greatness. Two people might seemingly be built the same and from similar backgrounds, but what makes one of them better at a sport than the other? God-given talent? Luck? Diet? Within all of that are the parents. You hear stories about the fathers of greats such as Tiger Woods and Andre Agassi being what some people might say was overly firm, but look at the genius they harboured. Thierry Henry has talked openly about his dad, who refused to praise him or say a simple, 'Well played'; was it mean or just clever tactics that spurred the Frenchman on to be the player he was?

I grew up with Frank Lampard and his dad was firm with him, but it got results. I watch a lot of kids' football today and I see the different methods, and it always makes me think of my dad, and our relationship not only with each other but with football itself. It's a fine balancing act.

Dad came everywhere to watch me play, but you wouldn't know it. You certainly didn't hear him. There were no histrionics, no screams of joy or frustration. What we did have, though, was a silent sign language. Just little hand and facial gestures that Dad would make from afar to let me know what he was thinking.

As a kid, I'd take a look, and there he was. What was on his mind? These were the options:

1. Pumps his arms quickly, legs too. This means do more, work more, run.
2. Claps his hands and rubs them together. This means we're in business. Keep doing what you're doing.
3. Grits his teeth and curls his lip. This means get physical, get stuck in.
4. Thumbs up. Simple but the best. This is the pinnacle and we're on for a Chinese tonight.

These gestures didn't change from the age of nine until thirty, and even when I was captain of Liverpool, an England international, I would glance up to the old Main Stand at Anfield, find my dad, and wonder which one would greet me.

All that seems long ago. Time passes. The knees get creakier, but the memories shine bright. Today, I am the old man on the sidelines and a new generation is falling in love with the game. And so it goes on. The passion remains. I guess it always will.

Chapter 1

Giants of the Game

HARRY

Growing up, Saturday was all about football. From August to May, Saturdays were spent with my dad and, whatever the weather, we were off to the match. Dad was a docker, but lived for football, and because of that I was lucky enough to witness some great footballers. Over the years, I have seen most of them. When we say 'greatness', I think of a moment back in the 1970s. We were living in America, and I was playing for the Seattle Sounders with Bobby Moore. Mooro was still one of the best players in the league and, in 1976, to mark the country's bicentennial celebrations, he was selected to play for Team America against Brazil, England and Italy.

It was after Bobby's game against Brazil. Team America had lost 2–0, and after the match, from the stands I noticed a player approach Rivelino. Now if we are talking greats, Rivelino was right up there, too. The most classy of Brazilian midfielders, one of their true greats, he had this fantastic stepover, could shoot, pass, took mind-boggling free-kicks and had the best moustache. The guy approaching him was a great lad called Keith Eddy who had played for Watford, and he asks if they can swap shirts. 'Fair play, Keith,' I'm thinking, 'that's some shirt to get.'

But then Rivelino shakes his head apologetically, and Keith is left empty handed. I'm feeling sorry for him when I notice the Brazilian begins to run upfield. He's running a good eighty yards towards Bobby, who is slowly walking from the pitch. Rivelino catches up with him, taps him on the shoulder, they talk, and Rivelino asks for his shirt, which Bobby of course gives him.

That's Rivelino, one of the truly great footballers of modern times, and he is running across a football pitch to get Bobby's shirt. That tells you everything about Mooro's greatness, a talent that I was lucky enough to see close up. That tells you everything about the great esteem Bobby Moore was held in, across the world.

JAMIE

I was lucky enough as a young boy to come to training and see Bobby close up, but I guess I was too young to

truly take in what a great he was. I just remember this very kind, polite man spending time with my family.

When it comes to my first experiences with greatness, like most sons, it would be my dad. Well, my dad and my grandad. People forget what a good player Dad was, but it was in his genes. My pops was some player. Harry Redknapp Snr. We used to go to the caravan on the Isle of Sheppey for our holidays, and play football all day, every day. Pops would be on the ball and I would look on with awe at his touch. He'd get on the ball, flick it up, juggle it with both feet, outside of the right, inside of the left, all these tricks, unbelievable. My uncle, Frank Lampard Snr, would join us. This is a West Ham player, an FA Cup winner, an international defender, and Pops would be nutmegging him.

Yeah, Dad was some player. He had unbelievable ability. My old man really should have been a professional, but like so many, the war years took that opportunity from him, and so when he came home from a prisoner-of-war camp, the chance was gone. He still had a great amateur career turning out for successful clubs such as Walthamstow Avenue. They were one of the biggest amateur sides in the country after the war, and Dad turned out for them, playing inside-forward. He was a class player, with a wonderful touch. Today I guess he'd be a classic number ten.

What I remember is the way the ball sounded when Dad and Pops struck it. It's stayed with me and it's the same way great footballers make the ball sound. It's different. Dad would strike the ball, and there was this sound. A ping. In 1998, when I was at Liverpool, Gérard Houllier brought a couple of kids over from the academy. One was Stephen Wright, a good defender with potential. Gérard wanted to see how he fared with the first team. With him, he brought a skinny looking kid called Steven Gerrard.

Wright did OK, but suddenly this lad called Gerrard hit a fifty-yard pass, but it was the sound it made. Like the ultimate golf shot, it just sounded perfect. Ping. Immediately he has my attention. Who is this kid? It was the noise. That familiar sound. Plus the way the greats like Stevie could make the ball fly through the air.

'What did you think of the youngster, Stephen Wright?' Houllier asked me after training.

'He's good,' I said. 'But what about the skinny lad? He's going to be some player.'

I would watch Dad and Pops, and notice the way the ball looked as if it wasn't spinning. I became fascinated with that. Today, Kevin De Bruyne does the same. Hits the ball with a pinging sound, the ball moves in that same special way. I look at today's greats and I definitely look for the things I noticed as a kid playing at our caravan. Growing up, my heroes became the players who looked

after the ball, who enjoyed having it at their feet, the players who protected possession.

My old man loved the same sort of players and would spend his time telling me all about the greats he had seen. Before the war, the exceptional footballers playing in London were players such as Hughie Gallacher at Chelsea and a fellow Scot, Alex James, at Arsenal. Both were great on the ball. Like him, neither were tall men, but they could play.

James was a legend at Arsenal, and Dad – even though he was from the East End – had started to follow the Arsenal. The thing is, back then, after the war, fans like him, while supporting one team (he also liked to take me to Millwall), would seek out greatness if it was in town. You might support one team, but if the likes of Stanley Matthews was around on a Saturday, you made a beeline to be there. The bus to Highbury or White Hart Lane, the Piccadilly Line down to Earl's Court to get to Stamford Bridge . . . it didn't matter, not when a great had come to play.

Everyone loved Stanley Matthews. He became football royalty, adored by the nation, but to my dad, Tom Finney was the greatest of that era. Sat in a pub, blokes might argue. Who's better, Stan or Tom? For my dad, and plenty of others, it was always Tom. He idolised him, and while he respected and loved Stanley, he felt that Finney was the better all-round player, able to play on the right-wing like Matthews, but he could also play across the front line, including at centre-forward or on the left.

Dad loved talking football and loved talking Finney, and he loved it when Preston were at Highbury. There, he would stand in the packed North Bank, with a flask of tea and some sandwiches. The thing is, there was no segregation back then, so Dad would usually get chatting to a gang of blokes who had come down from Lancashire for the match. They'd talk about the journey down, 'Left on the five a.m. train and changed at Bolton . . .' before Dad would ask about how Tom was playing that season. Dad would pour the tea, and they'd all stand there and chat. Never any aggro. It was after the war, and I suppose the public were just so happy to be back watching proper football, watching proper greats. Both had been denied them for so long.

Another of Dad's great idols was Jimmy Logie. Another Scot, another talented inside-forward. Jimmy had joined Arsenal the year the war broke out, so it wasn't until the 1940s that he got to really appreciate his talent. Jimmy was a key player in 1950 when Arsenal won the FA Cup, setting up both goals in a 2–0 win against Liverpool. He scored plenty of goals too, and Dad never stopped talking about him. When Jimmy retired from football, he would sell newspapers near the Arsenal stadium.

Dad would take me to the match, we would get off at Finsbury Park, and each time, we would walk to the ground making sure to go past Jimmy's little newsstand. Even if Dad didn't need a paper, he would stop to say hello, have a little chat about that day's game, because that was the great Jimmy Logie. I always remember him, this great of the post-war game, wearing an old mackintosh tied up around the waist with a long piece of string. He was always so friendly, and loved to talk about football. It's mad to think that only a few seasons earlier, Jimmy had been the star turn at the stadium by which he was now selling the early evening news.

When I started to really take it all in, in the mid- and late 1950s, Arsenal didn't have the best team. They had great players, though, like Jack Kelsey, the Welsh goalkeeper. David Herd was a superb forward at Highbury who would go on and play for Matt Busby's glorious Manchester United side in the 1960s. Geoff Strong was a brilliant midfielder too but, like Herd, he left, and played under Bill Shankly at Liverpool.

One day stands out, and that was the day the Busby Babes came to town. That was a special but, as it turned out, also a very sad day. It was the first day of February 1958. Manchester United were coming to Highbury, but it would be the last time they played on English soil before the tragedy of their aeroplane's crash in Munich just a few days later.

They were the league champions, for two consecutive seasons. They were young, and everyone wanted to watch them. For me, though, the main draw was Duncan Edwards. I was eleven years old and this young man, at twenty-one years old, was already achieving so much in the game. He was the talk of the town.

I remember my eyes were transfixed on him. I was so jealous of the young boy, about my age, who was the mascot that day. He got to kick a ball about with Duncan Edwards and, most annoyingly, he got to have his hair ruffled by him.

Duncan, in the flesh, stood out. He was colossal. He would dominate games. We had heard stories about him, stories about his days playing in the Manchester United youth team, a man among boys. It was said that, in Youth Cup games, they would play him up front in the first half, let him score a hat-trick, and then, in the second half, they'd stick him at centre-half to keep the lead.

Alongside him was Bobby Charlton, one of the true greats. Bobby was already known around the country as a great young player, and one that so many clubs wanted to sign. He was a modest man, but he knew he had talent as a young schoolboy footballer, he thought he could play a bit, but he said that back then, when he arrived at Manchester United and saw Duncan training, well, maybe he wasn't as good as he hoped. For Bobby Charlton, arguably England's greatest ever player to say that, well that tells you something about the talent Duncan had, and the talent that was so sadly taken from us.

The Munich air crash was a tragedy, a sad shock for everyone, and so many lives were taken. It transcends football really and the whole country felt it. Duncan's death was part of all that, but years later we can only speculate about what his career might have looked like.

He was already one of the best players – if not the best – in the league when he died. He had everything. He looked so powerful, his legs were bigger and stronger than players of his era, he could pass, shoot, head. Sadly, it's only speculation, but in 1966 he would have not yet been thirty years old, so I think he would have been part of Alf Ramsey's squad that won the World Cup. I'm not sure where he would have played, maybe at centre-back with Mooro. Imagine that? I reckon that he would have been a dynamic box-to-box midfielder though. Alongside Charlton in there, marauding around the pitch. He might have man-marked Franz Beckenbauer, allowing Charlton to attack a bit more. We'll never know, but it's some thought. What I do believe is that Duncan Edwards would have gone down as one of the all-time greats . . . and by that I mean world greats.

That's how good he was. He would have been one of the game's true stars. Bobby Charlton is rightly thought of that way, and if the great man felt inferior to Duncan, well, that says it all doesn't it?

I love watching footage of Bobby Charlton. I remember going to his soccer school in Manchester when I was a boy

and, even then, us kids were in awe of him and his career. It was the way he glided across the pitch. The World Cup in England, the biggest games in England's history, and there was Bobby, at the forefront of it all, moving across the pitch, seemingly without a care in the world. But then he would drop his shoulder, send the world's best defenders for a hot dog, and smash the ball into the top corner. The goals against Mexico and then Portugal in the semi-final . . . wow! He's just an icon, isn't he? Even the hair. He somehow made the combover look cool. Having said that, if he was playing today, he would have headed to Turkey by now and been playing with a full barnet.

If we are talking *the* greats, I can't think of a better English footballer. Ever. Bobby just did it all, at club and international level, and he has to be England's greatest player.

Bobby Charlton was special. A special player and a special man. He was like poetry. It was so graceful to watch, and he would unleash that thunderbolt of a shot. From either foot, wallop, he would strike the ball and it would usually fly, seemingly without spinning, into the top corner of the net. Off the pitch, like Bobby Moore, he was a class act. These guys never went round mouthing off or kicking anyone. They just oozed class.

To share a pitch with Bobby Charlton . . . well, that was both a pleasure and, if I am honest, a bit of a pain. I was in midfield against him, and it wasn't easy. He had this speed of thought. I remember one match at Upton Park in 1967. Manchester United were going for the title (which they would win) and Bobby, from the off, was all over us. He scored with his first shot, a typical wonder strike, and I have to admit, while I tried to compete with him in that midfield, like so many of us, I was probably a bit in awe of him.

When he hit the ball, it sounded like church bells. I agree that he must be up there as England's best, but the 1960s gave us so many great midfielders and if you are drawn to players who liked to look after the ball, players who could keep the ball and pass the ball, well, I'll tell you who you would have loved: Johnny Haynes of Fulham and England.

Johnny Haynes was an immaculate footballer. My dad certainly loved him. He had that easy way about him, that ability to tide the game over. Possession, possession, possession. At the time, he was the cleanest passer of the ball around. In the late 1950s and early 1960s, his passing was second to none. He had this reverse pass. Johnny would be on the ball, running one way, but his vision meant that he could see what was on, and he would switch play some forty-five yards, dropping the ball on a sixpence at the feet of a teammate. Pelé called him the greatest passer of the ball he'd ever seen. That can't be bad, can it?

He also looked good, always in a great suit. Johnny was among the first footballers to do advertising when he became the face of Brylcreem. He was also the first player to earn a few bob. When football's maximum wage was abolished in 1961, Haynes was clever. His chairman at Fulham was the famous comedian, Tommy Trinder. Tommy was a great character, he loved to hold court, and would tell anyone who would listen that he would gladly pay a hundred quid to watch his star player, Johnny Haynes.

So, when the day came that the maximum weekly wage of £20 came to an end, Johnny rightly and quickly headed to Tommy's office at Craven Cottage.

'Hello, Mr Chairman.'

'Hello, Johnny. What can I do for you?'

'You can put your money where your mouth is: pay up that hundred quid you've always gone on about.'

That was that, Johnny was the first player on a oner a week.

Even with a bit of cash in their back pockets, Johnny and the rest of the lads back then were such a modest bunch, and football then really wasn't about playing well and trying to get a big move. Usually, you came through the youth ranks, made the first team, and that was you until the club decided they wanted to sell you.

The one that did get a big move away when he was young was Jimmy Greaves. Put simply, Greavsie was the best finisher I have ever seen. I loved Jimmy. The most charming, unassuming man and, from the age of seventeen, the best striker around. He did get that big money move to Italy, when he joined AC Milan in 1961, unheard of back then.

The great players in my day were discovered by scouts. Scouts were as influential as agents are now, and if and when a promising young talent turned up, they went to great lengths to make sure their club benefited. At West Ham, we had a fella called Charlie Faulkner. He signed me, so he must have been good!

Charlie was a real good bloke, and a great character. At West Ham, I played with a great forward called John Sissons. We won the 1963 Youth Cup final together, beating Liverpool, and he went on to score in the following year's FA Cup final, becoming the then youngest to do so. He was some talent, and had been spotted by Charlie playing for Middlesex Schoolboys, but Charlie and West Ham had a problem. Everyone wanted John.

Everyone wanted him, but not everyone was as clever as Charlie. He got talking to John's parents' neighbour. He put this guy on the West Ham payroll, and asked him to work for him. The job? Well, this guy had to keep his eyes out for visitors to the Sissons' home. If anyone came by, anyone he didn't know to be immediate family or friends, Charlie was to be phoned. And that's what the neighbour did. Every time some bloke turned up, usually a scout from Arsenal, Spurs, Chelsea or whoever, Charlie got called, and he would get in his car, be at the house and sitting in with them so nothing could be seriously talked about. Basically, he naused it up for everyone else until West Ham made the signing.

It was another scout who spotted a slightly chubby little wing-half called Robert Moore. That was a local scout called Jack Turner along with West Ham's chief scout, a fella called Wally St Pier. Between them they spotted him playing schoolboy football, and got him to join the club as an apprentice, but credit for Mooro has to go with their former centre-half, Malcolm Allison. Malcolm had been a great player but his career was shortened due to an illness, and it was as a young, budding coach that he made one of the biggest contributions to English football.

Mooro would often say it: without Malcolm he would not have been the player he was. Bobby was a good young player, but no one saw true greatness in him. Well, no one except Malcolm. It sounds crazy but West Ham were considering not taking Bobby on. Can you imagine that? There were people at the club who thought Bobby was a bit of a plodder, a half-decent footballer at best, but probably not worth having one of their sought-after pro contracts.

Only one of those contracts remained, and it was going to go to Bobby or another lad. The report on Mooro was far from enthusiastic. Not very tall, not very quick, not very good in the air, not a great runner. Malcolm had taken the kids' teams and wasn't having any of that. 'He's going to be a player,' Malcolm said to anyone who would listen and, thankfully, someone did, because Bobby got the contract.

Malcolm saw something different from sheer athleticism. He saw a football brain, a kid who listened and understood how the game worked. He saw a young kid who might be more than simply a bruising stopper centre-half. Bobby used to tell me a story that summed it up. Mooro was playing in a youth-team game at the training ground, against Chelsea. Chelsea had Barry Bridges up front. Barry was quality and had already played first-team football. Bobby stuck to Barry like Sellotape. Everywhere the Chelsea striker went, Bobby was there too, and the game finished 0–0.

After the match, Bobby went in, thinking, here we go, Malcolm is going to be well happy with me, but instead he gets to the dressing room and Malcolm has a face like thunder. He is furious and lays into him. 'Play like that again, and I will never talk to you again, do you hear?' he said.

Bobby was confused, so Malcolm explained.

'When our keeper had the ball, where were you? You were looking at Barry bloody Bridges, that's where. I've told you, we build from the back and that means you being available to take the ball from him, or giving your full-back an angle, looking for the ball and starting our attacks. We did none of that today because you didn't. I'm serious, if you play like that again, you won't be getting any more help from me.'

Well, Bobby listened, didn't he, and built a magnificent career on doing exactly what Malcolm said to do, but not even Malcolm's sharp eye could have known just how brilliantly he'd do it. The thing is, that initial report on Bobby as a boy was kind of accurate. He wasn't that big, just five feet eleven, he wasn't quick, and he wouldn't head the ball much. But he didn't need pace because he was always where the ball was; he wasn't the biggest but no one ever got the better of him physically; and he didn't need to head the ball because, well, why should he?

He'd mark these giant centre-forwards. Guys like Wyn Davies, a big Welshman at Bolton and Newcastle. Bobby would mark Wyn, the long goal-kick would be launched, Bobby would move with Wyn, fake to jump with him, but then gently drop off, Wyn would flick the ball on, and there's Bobby, twenty feet back receiving the ball on his chest before casually but decisively playing the ball forward to a teammate.

Look at how Mooro played in Mexico in 1970. Young defenders should still watch his games out there against some of the best strikers of all time, because he's so precise, so clean in his defending. That tackle against Jairzinho? The Brazilian is running at him at pace, and Bobby is brave, brave enough to wait, brave enough to let him come into the box, waiting for the opportunity. And then he's in, clean as a whistle, taking the ball and starting an attack. He used to do that to all of us in training. Every single day.

Today, I have a giant framed photo in my house. It's the iconic shot of Bobby embracing Pelé after that Brazil game in 1970, and all you can see is mutual respect. It's no surprise. Bobby wasn't some flash in the pan. Being photographed in an embrace with Pelé was natural, because Mooro was right up there alongside the greats of the game.

I love hearing about Bobby. It's strange for me, because I was in the very fortunate and unique position of knowing Bobby Moore simply as Uncle Bobby, my dad's mate. Having Bobby around was normal but, even as a kid, I could tell there was this aura to him. He was always the most famous man in the room, but he had time for everyone. He was one of the chaps, one of the boys, polite to all the wives, to waiters, to bar staff and to us boys. He would take me and my brother Mark to the garden, and kick a ball about with us. How lucky was I? The greatest England captain of all time and I'm getting a pass from him on the lawn. Even then, towards the end of his career, you could tell by the way he played with us that he just loved football. Bobby always looked great too, didn't he? I loved how Dad would describe him as a roommate. All his clothes folded perfectly, even his underpants and socks immaculately pressed.

We also had George Best over a lot. He would stay at ours. George was always happy to play out in the garden with us boys. In fact, I'd say he was happiest when a ball

was at his feet. Mark and I would compete to show off in front of this genius of a footballer. We'd be out there doing our keepy-ups, we'd pass using both feet, but then watch in awe as he would show us some of the magic he still possessed.

Well, my boys were playing with, in my opinion, the greatest footballer Britain has ever produced. It's that simple. George was so talented, so naturally gifted. I remember West Ham going up to Old Trafford. It was 1971. I got some intel from one of the United lads that George had been out all night with a girl, that he'd had no sleep, and catching sight of him, he was not looking his best. I strolled into our dressing room full of it.

'Good news, lads, George is out of it,' I crowed. 'He's playing, but only coz they ain't got anyone else.'

Our boys went out with a spring in their steps, but came in with their tails between their legs. We lost 4–2 and George got a hat-trick. 'Good tip, Harry,' the lads said.

What you have to remember is that George was playing at a time when defenders were allowed to carry out actual bodily harm on forwards and did so with relish. George was the finest dribbler of the ball we'd ever seen, but did it through mud, and facing the likes of Ron Harris at Chelsea who would try to cut him in half. However, with a swivel of his hips, with bravery and with his own strength, he would ride the challenge and be away.

It was the same for Pelé. Like George, the great Brazilian forward faced medieval-style challenges, and like George could ride tackles like an Olympic hurdler. Look at his physique: he was like a middleweight boxer. I remember him coming into all our lives. It was 1958, when we heard reports and saw clips of this seventeen-year-old Brazilian kid dominating the World Cup out in Sweden. What a player, what a career. If someone says to me that Pelé is the greatest footballer of all time, they'll get no argument from me.

That must have been crazy. I love those clips. The goals he scored in the tournament are incredible. He scores one in the quarter-finals, a hat-trick in the semi-finals against France and then two in the final against the hosts, Sweden. Can you imagine today, if a seventeen-year-old came on to the scene, and at a World Cup performed like that? His life would be nuts. Look at the Spanish kid, Lamine Yamal. At the 2024 European Championship in Germany, he scores a wonder goal, and everyone is talking about him. Pelé, at a similar age, scores six in three games.

Dad always said what a humble guy Pelé was, and I remember him coming home having played against him out in America, and he had left his mark on Dad. The Seattle Sounders were playing Pelé's New York Cosmos, and they used that Adidas ball, one with a red star on a blue hexagon. The Brazilian was heading for goal, and

Dad, always the brave player, threw his leg in front of a fierce shot from Pelé; he blocks it but he's in agony, and the ball has left its mark on his thigh.

I remember Dad coming home a couple of hours later, and there it is, the print still on his leg. That star on a hexagon. I was so impressed. Not with Dad's defending prowess, but that it was the great Pelé who put it there. I was always wanting to hear about him. He seemed to me, when I was very young and despite the fact that I never saw him play live, to be *the* great. I couldn't get enough of Dad's stories about him. Even his goal in the film *Escape to Victory* seemed to be greater than anything we'd ever seen. But, in time, as I grew older I started to choose my own heroes.

I think the turning point for me was the 1982 World Cup. I think that was the summer I truly fell in love with the global game. I loved football before that, but it was watching those games in Spain that changed a lot for me. As much as I already admired players playing in the English First Division, players like Glenn Hoddle and Bryan Robson, it was seeing the likes of Michel Platini and Jean Tigana with France and Zico, Falcão, Éder and Sócrates with Brazil that opened my eyes.

I had heard all about Brazil from Dad. I had watched a few clips of old players and great goals, but to watch that iconic yellow kit live on TV and those players, playing a style of football we had never seen, it all just clicked.

We'd watch Sócrates dropping a shoulder, Éder chipping the keeper, Falcão shooting from distance, but it was Zico that I wanted to be. That's what these great players do for kids. We all want to try to emulate them when we watch World Cups. After Marco Tardelli's iconic goal in the 1982 final, I went out and worked hard on shooting with my left foot. Zico's skills too. He could do the rabona trick but, to be fair to Dad, I had already seen that. I'm not joking, Dad was great at that trick. He reckons he still is.

If the 1982 World Cup made me fall in love with the game, then the 1986 competition made me infatuated. I was almost twelve by then, and loved every minute. The Azteca ball, the amount of goals from long range. Something that I always wanted to do. Players that seemed so exotic. The likes of Enzo Francescoli of Uruguay, Preben Elkjær and Michael Laudrup of Denmark in that Hummel kit, I couldn't get enough. But it was Diego Maradona that summer that changed the football world, wasn't it?

We knew all about Maradona before the 1982 World Cup but he struggled to shine there, thanks largely to the Italian defender Claudio Gentile, who man-marked him in what you could describe as an aggressive manner. The thing is, Gentile was only doing what so many 'hard men' were doing and, to be fair, they were only doing what they were allowed to do. That's what made the likes of Maradona and Pelé so great. George Best too. Not only were they the most complete footballers we'd seen, but they were doing it on terrible pitches against players who were encouraged to stop them, even if that meant using violence.

Gentile kicked the shit out of Maradona, that day. Eleven fouls in the first half, twelve in the second, and that's just the ones the referee blew up for. He properly kicked him. I think I once read the Italian defender say, 'Football's not for ballerinas.' Well, Maradona was no ballerina but even he was going to struggle against that sort of behaviour.

Those rules, and the sheer physicality of the game, make it so hard to compare those playing today and those playing back then. I think you can only talk about the greatest players of each generation. The rules have changed too much, pitches have improved too much. What is certain to me, though, is that summer in 1986 Maradona gave the planet the greatest ever individual World Cup performance.

That performance against England in the quarter-final? Wow. Yes, there was that rascal side of his character on show with the first goal but even that fascinated me. How has he thought so quickly and looked so innocent? Don't get me wrong, it was cheating, but I admired how hellbent he was on winning.

As for the second goal . . . the turn, the way the ball is under his command, the midfielders and defenders just not able to get near him, the ability to get around Peter Shilton and remain in control of the football, I had never seen anything like it. I remember after the game talking to Dad at the dinner table. All our chat was about the skill on show. We didn't really talk about the handball, I just wanted to discuss Maradona's ability. I think Dad was upset that John Barnes hadn't got on earlier too. Always the manager!

By then I was managing at Bournemouth, and if we are talking about great players, we shouldn't just limit it to the very top and those who shone at World Cups. The lower leagues were, and still are, full of great footballers.

Players like Ian Bishop. Bish was a great footballer. We scouted him at Carlisle and signed him for twenty grand in 1988. He played a season or so with us and we sold him to Manchester City for £750,000. That's what it was all about. Looking for great players for no money and selling them to keep a club like Bournemouth afloat.

We once got a young defender from non-league Weymouth. I liked him immediately and fought to get the £50,000 to sign him in 1989. He did great for us. His name was Stuart Teale. In 1991, the family were on holiday in Majorca. Me, Sandra, Mark and Jamie are walking along the seafront, when I hear a shout.

'Harry! Harry!'

It's Ron Atkinson. Ron has just become manager at Aston Villa. We all go over, and Ron is saying, 'Sit down, join us for a drink.'

We all sit down and soon talk, as ever, turns to football. Ron tells me he is looking for a new centre-half. 'Harry, who is the best centre-back in the lower leagues?'

'Shaun Teale,' I say without hesitation.

'Who does he play for?' Ron asks.

'Bournemouth.'

'I'm not falling for that,' Ron says. 'You're trying to offload one of your crap players.'

'Ron, I am telling you. This lad is quick, only five feet eleven but with an unbelievable spring, a terrific left foot. You asked me a question, and I am giving you an answer. He's top drawer.'

Ron's not convinced and we part ways, and then, back in England, I get a call. It's Ron.

'All right, Harry, I have asked about, and you were right. It seems your player is as good as you say. How much?'

'Half a million quid, Ron.'

'All right, I'll have him.'

On the first day of the following season, Villa beat Sheffield Wednesday and Shaun Teale is the man of the match. We're on our way back from somewhere like Stockport and have the coach radio on. 'Right, let's go to Villa Park where we have Ron Atkinson ready to talk.'

Ron comes on and is asked about his new centre-half.

'Yeah, as soon as I saw him playing at Bournemouth I knew he had talent. There was no doubt in my mind that this was a lad who could play in the top flight.'

I sat there on the coach laughing my head off. I love Big Ron, but he had no idea how good Stuart was.

Even today, players learn so much in the lower leagues. I loved watching Crystal Palace recently because I liked to watch Eberechi Eze and Michael Olise, before he left for Bayern Munich. Both would try things, tricks, and they learned that by playing in the Championship.

Even when Jamie was sixteen, I threw him on at Bournemouth and knew he'd learn so much when I did. But when a great like Kenny Dalglish at Liverpool calls asking to sign your son, it's tricky. I did tell him that Jamie wanted to play first-team football, but with reports from his scout, Ron Yeats, he was adamant and told me he would be in and around the team. When Jamie went to up to meet him, I knew he was in good hands.

I had been at Tottenham but when they offered me schoolboy forms, I didn't fancy it. I wanted to play first-team football. I was only sixteen, and that might sound mad, but I just felt that I would learn more playing league football with Dad at Bournemouth, so I turned them down. I think Dad thought I was a bit mad but he put me in, and I did, I learned so much.

When Liverpool showed an interest a year later, in 1991, I was so excited to meet Kenny. I had known him as one of the truly great British players. I arrived at Anfield, aged sixteen, to talk to him, and the first thing I did was run to the club shop, buy a photo of him, and I asked him to sign it. 'Dear Jamie, See you soon, Kenny Dalglish.' He was so kind to me, having me stay at his house. I was a bit starstruck but he couldn't have been nicer.

It was all a bit of a coincidence because, when he was a schoolboy, Kenny came to West Ham, and Ron Greenwood asked me to pick him and another lad up every morning to bring them to training. He had come for a trial, but really it was West Ham who were on trial. Kenny was the most sought-after schoolboy in British football, and when we watched him play we could see why.

One Saturday morning, Ron put him into a practice game. First team versus the reserves. Kenny gets the ball, back to goal, and scores that goal he scored so many times. He gets it, backs into the defender, spins him, feints, curls it into the top corner with his left foot. We all stopped and applauded. Literally applauded. We all asked Ron if we had any hope of getting him. 'No chance,' he said. I did used to pick him up in my first little car though.

He was just as good in training over twenty years later when I arrived at Liverpool. It is always an eye-opener

getting close up to truly great players. I had been at Spurs and played a bit with Glenn Hoddle. That was something. The ease in which he could play. Naturally two-footed, able to bring the ball down from anywhere. To be around that sort of talent, close up, that's when you see just how great these guys are. Even when I was an international footballer, I had that sort of experience on the pitch when we played France at Wembley in 1999.

They had Emmanuel Petit and Didier Deschamps, but it was Zinedine Zidane I was interested in. I'm not going to lie, I was in awe of him, maybe a bit like Dad was when he faced Bobby Charlton. I didn't want to get too close for fear of him taking the piss. It's hard to explain how good he was. He was so big, huge feet, physical, but his touch . . . oh, his touch was the best I have ever seen. The ball was under his spell the whole time. At half-time, walking off, I did something I had never done before or since. I went up to Zidane and asked if, at the end of the game, we could swap shirts. He smiled and agreed.

With two minutes left, I get subbed, and I think that's that, especially as I notice David Beckham is man-marking him for the last two minutes. The game ends, I'm walking from the Wembley pitch when I hear, 'Jamie, Jamie.' I turn around and it's Zidane.

'We swap shirts now?'

The idea that not only had he remembered but that he knew my name? It all sounds like I was a fanboy, but it

was just huge admiration and respect for his ability. I still have the shirt. Or my son does!

I was always interested in the players Jamie played with and against. And not because I was secretly scouting them. Sir Alex Ferguson used to do the same to me, phoning me wanting to know about any great players I might have. First time he did it was around 2001 regarding Paolo Di Canio. Paolo was superb for me, and I had left West Ham when Fergie rang about him. I told him to sign Paolo, thinking he'd be great for United. He had the personality, like Eric Cantona, to do great there. I don't why, but he didn't take my advice.

The other time was in 2011, the morning after the Champions League final, when I was at Tottenham. Fergie's team had just been soundly beaten by a Barcelona housing some of the true greats. Iniesta, Xavi, Messi; they'd out-passed United, and Fergie must have realised that night how much the game was changing, and what teams like his now needed. He called me immediately, first thing next morning, and asked about Luka Modrić. Sell Luka? That wasn't going to happen, not then, not to United, but I could see why he did it.

Luka was the most incredible guy, never a problem, a family man, one of the truly great footballers. The players used to start training with a game of piggy-in-the-middle. I think they now call it rondo. One day it hit me, and I said, 'Luka, I have been with you for three years and I have never seen you in the middle.' He just smiled but it was true, he never ever gave the ball away.

What about Lionel Messi? When discussing the greats, the Argentinian and Cristiano Ronaldo are always on everyone's lips. The debate about who is the better player has defined a generation. I think both myself and Dad are Messi fans, but you can't disregard Ronaldo. What a player. I remember playing against Ronaldo when he was at Manchester United. It was his first season. We lost 2–0 and after the game Fergie came over to me for a chat.

'How's your dad?' and all that.

I then said to him, 'Cor, that new winger of yours is some player.'

'Give it three years,' Fergie said. 'He'll be the best in the world.'

Fergie wasn't far off with that prediction, but I think Messi pips him. Messi was such a special player. At his peak, I took my son, Charley, to see him play for Barcelona against Real Madrid in the Bernabéu. Messi takes on half the team, scores a quite beautiful goal, and even the home fans are up applauding. To be there live, with my boy, it was a special moment. It's like watching Federer dominate Centre Court or Tiger Woods marching along the fairway at Augusta. Seeing true greatness like that transcends sport, and to have that moment with Charley was special.

Messi and Ronaldo are both right up there with the all-time greats, but for me Messi is the best. It is so hard, though, so hard to compare generations. The rule changes, the pitches and the laws of the game. They've changed so drastically. How can anyone know how the likes of Messi and Ronaldo would have coped in the mud, or against Claudio Gentile?

I think what we can say without doubt is that if we put Pelé or George Best or Maradona on today's pitches and tell them that defenders are hardly allowed any physical contact, well it is 100 per cent certain that they would excel. Would the modern greats have been able to do it on mud-bath pitches when faced with defenders who knew that any tackle below the throat was legal? Dad's right, we'll never know.

What I am concerned about in the modern game is the lack of spontaneous talent. Players who like the true greats are able to produce something out of nothing. Where are those players? Jude Bellingham is some talent, but there are very few remarkable kids coming through out there. Look at the last European Championship in Germany. Rodri was player of the tournament. Don't get me wrong, he is a world-class footballer but he is a holding midfielder, hardly one to get you off your feet.

Today, the academies are incredible. State of the art. But are they producing great players? I don't think so. I visited the Bournemouth academy recently to see my grandson. A young boy caught my eye. Very young, but very talented. He was trying tricks. He was dribbling, trying drag-backs, Cruyff turns. In one moment, he lost the ball. The coach screamed at him, telling him to not risk losing possession. He screamed at him to pass the ball. Pass, pass, pass. The parents are joining in and I'm standing there thinking, let the boy try his tricks, let the boy be inventive. It really worried me.

Let's hope that's not the norm and that this generation can bring football fans as much pleasure as the players who made me fall in love with the game. We'll never settle the argument about who the greatest of all time is, so I'll settle on it being my dad. Well, Dad and Pops.

Chapter 2

1966 and All That

HARRY

They ended up in a dark corner, out of any limelight and next to the facilities. It was Danny La Rue's. A popular nightclub belonging to the famous drag and cabaret act, on the West End's Hanover Square. Not a place I knew, being only nineteen then with a social life that still didn't expand past Whitechapel. Bobby Moore, however, the centre-half, the skipper, and arguably the most famous man in the country, he knew a lot of places, and this was the club that sprang to his mind, the night England won the World Cup.

The squad, all of them the best of young men, had returned triumphantly from Wembley to a plush hotel on Kensington High Street. Thousands of people lined the streets, singing and cheering, hoping to catch a glimpse of the men who, just hours earlier, had made England champions of the world. People clung on to lampposts, got on friends' shoulders, climbed up on bus stops and cheered on the lads, gleefully admiring the small but glorious Jules Rimet trophy shining under a sea of photographers' lights.

That evening, the Football Association threw the team a gala dinner – albeit one to which the players' wives were not invited and had to instead enjoy their own modest supper in some hotel backroom – and with those 'niceties' over, Bobby told anyone wanting to take the party into the London night that he knew a place.

Bobby, the team's captain in more ways than one, made a phone call from their hotel, a table was reserved and, with a few of the lads and their now welcome wives, he headed west. They arrived without a fanfare, just the way they liked it, headed into the cabaret club, and then they were shown to their table. A group of young men, who have just won England the World Cup, walking almost unnoticed through a candlelit room, and shown to a dingy table at the back of the club, right next to the toilets. Madness.

That's what happened to many of the lads that night. That's how they were treated. If you can't imagine that happening today, that's because it wouldn't. Today, should the national team ever match that of the boys of '66, you can be sure that both the FA and the owners of every

West End institution they chose to party in would treat them like kings.

Not that the guys who won England's only major football trophy wanted or sought regal status. Far from it. By the time Bobby was wiping the mud from his hands so he could shake the queen's without dirtying her pristine, white gloves, I had broken into the West Ham first team, even scoring my first goal at Tottenham, and had become great pals with the West Ham lads who so influenced England's glory that summer.

I knew plenty of the other guys in the squad and would go on to call several of them close mates, and what is certain is that they were the most down-to-earth set you could ever meet. Just a normal bunch of lads, all having grown up in post-war Britain, playing with pals among the country's bombsites, finding their talent with a ball until, on that day, they were on top of the world.

For me, in my late teens, it was as if I had arrived in the centre of the universe. A professional footballer, still living with my parents in the East End, playing the game I loved with my mates, enjoying a beer or two, and all in a city that was now the most famous on the planet.

London in the mid-1960s was the epicentre of the world. Cool Britannia. Fashion, music, cinema and eventually football, all eyes were on our country. Being in and among that West Ham team was a dream. The team had won the European Cup Winners' Cup in 1965, and it was that August that I was given my first-team debut, a night match at Upton Park against Sunderland. Martin Peters scored our goal in a 1–1 draw. I must have done OK, as I was picked the following Saturday, against a very good Leeds team, and we won 2–1.

It was a dream. I was getting a wage while playing football with my mates, all of whom came from exactly the same type of place that I did. We were council estate boys from all over London and the south-east. We all looked at life the same way, shared the same sense of humour, and so it was football and laughs all the way. By the time I began to play first-team football, I already knew the senior lads well. That's how it was at West Ham. The manager, Ron Greenwood, made sure of that in the way that the youth team and the first team were always integrated. When we were playing in the Youth Cup, we were very aware that Bobby was watching and with him was Ken Brown and Geoff Hurst or whoever else. By the time we came into the first-team dressing room, they were already treating us as equals.

We'd all go to the pub together after training. Nothing crazy, just a few pints and a laugh in the pubs around Chigwell. Bobby was always at the heart of it, and if things did get a bit out of hand, he had the answers. These were different times, but the police were still prone to stopping cars in the evening hoping to catch out drivers who might have had one too many. Bobby bought a chauffeur's hat, suggesting that the police wouldn't pull over a chauffeur-driven car, and so, if we'd had a half a shandy too many, he would stick the hat on, get us in the back of his car and drive us home.

Saturday nights were extra special and, without fail, us boys would be out in the pubs, each one of us wearing the suit we'd taken extra care to save for and buy. Those were the rules. You had to have a good suit. All of us lads, we'd head to Max Cohen in Aldgate or Phil Segal in Poplar, the best tailors around. We got our suits made to measure, mohair, nice cuts, and on a Saturday night, on they went. Shirt and tie, our shoes like mirrors, and we were off. The girls too, they got dressed up to the nines, and we'd all get together in the pubs. They were packed. Everyone having the best time, all the sixties music, bit of Motown; all great memories.

One of my prized possessions was a Crombie my dad had got me when I was just about sixteen. We walked from our estate in Poplar all the way to Aldgate and got me this overcoat. It was a cold winter but putting this overcoat on was like wearing armour. It was so, so heavy. I could hardly lift it. It took some effort to even walk in it. I loved that coat. I still have it somewhere. In fact, I think my son Mark was the last to have his hands on it.

Everyone looked good, but no one better than Bobby. He was the guvnor. If Bobby came into training or came out with us wearing something new, us younger lads were all over it, trying to find out where we could get our hands on whatever he had. He had this way about him, never affected by his fame or his position as England captain, even with the 1966 World Cup coming up, and wherever he went, he had time for people, and you could see how happy that time made them. Usually.

There was this one bloke. We had played away at Wolverhampton and come back into town, and myself, Frank Lampard Snr and Bobby popped into the Blind Beggar pub in Whitechapel. It was a very popular place with us players, Bobby was a long-time pal of the owners, two brothers called Patsy and Jimmy Quill. Great lads.

The pub also attracted the local gangsters. It was the pub in which Ronnie Kray shot George Cornell in March 1966, but we never saw any violence. Even most of the local hard men would be in awe of seeing Bobby but then, on this night, I walked into the loo, and in follows a big guy, long overcoat on, and a menacing-looking scar across his cheek.

'You tell your mate, Bobby Moore, that I'm gonna cut him from here to here,' he said, pointing from his ear to his mouth.

'Why?' I asked, shocked as I'd never heard anyone say something bad about Bobby, let alone threatening.

'Coz I don't like him,' he said. 'He fancies himself too much. He thinks he's a bit of a film star.'

I didn't tell Bobby but made sure we all got out of there quick, before telling him the following morning.

News got back to Jimmy Quill. Both brothers were football mad and they loved Bobby. Jimmy, an ex-boxer, was having none of it. 'He's a mug,' Jimmy said about the guy who meant Bobby harm. I don't know exactly what happened, but I heard that this supposed gangster was taken to one side by Jimmy and, with a combination of actions and words, convinced never to come back.

I was still a teenager living on the same estate with my parents but, thanks to football, us very ordinary lads were living extraordinary lives . . .

JAMIE

I was never a big West Ham fan. Dad had played for them so I liked them, and Mark was a massive fan, but I never fully committed. Too busy playing probably, but I always, always understood and respected their part in England winning the 1966 World Cup. It was weird, because I knew all three: Bobby Moore, Geoff Hurst and Martin Peters, and in the case of Bobby and Geoff, who had been out in Seattle with us as kids just ten years after that glorious summer, I'd spent a lot of time with them.

Yes, they were ordinary guys, and yes, none of them had any conceit or airs and graces, but from that young age, being among them, I was very aware of the magnitude of what they had achieved and the awe in which they were held. You just had to be in a busy room and notice the

slight hush when one of Geoff or Bobby walked in. Neither played on it, or even noticed it I would imagine, but it was there. These were the men who had won the World Cup. In our country, that is like walking on the moon, and you can't blame anyone for feeling that sense of reverence.

As a boy, I would ask Dad about it, what it was like to see the country win, who had been the best players, and then as I got older, my obsession firmly in place, I'd watch footage, loving the famous red shirts we wore in the final, wondering what the iconic orange ball must have been like to strike, convincing myself that the third goal crossed the line (it must have!), and then shooting at our little nets in the garden, whilst copying Ken Wolstenholme's famous line, 'It is now!'

Dad loved talking about it. Bobby Charlton, a goal-scoring midfielder . . . tell me more. I'd devour the stories and marvel at the footage. The way he glided across the pitch, that ability to strike a ball that according to my old man weighed a ton when wet, but was somehow always lightened by Bobby's ability. Then there was Alan Ball, a player who became a firm friend of Dad's and lived near us on the south coast. What a player he was and what a tournament he had. Such a fine footballer.

The whole thing became ingrained in me. I loved football, I loved English football, I was a sponge for knowledge about both, and so that summer of '66 was the pinnacle, and because my dad had experienced it while playing for West Ham, it felt closer, like somehow I had an affiliation with it.

The manager too. Sir Alf Ramsey seemed like this distant, godlike figure. The man who had led England to the World Cup. The only man who ever had. Looking back on what he did and how he did it, you have to admire his single-mindedness. He did things his way. The tactics. A 4–2–4 formation with flying wingers is all the rage, but Alf looks at his squad and thinks, no. Let's do this differently.

He picks a team with what today would be labelled inverted wide men, allowing Bobby Charlton to move forward. A 4–3–3 or a midfield diamond, depending on your point of view. And then there was the issue of Jimmy Greaves, the country's great goalscorer, the best in the country at it, the man to lead the country to victory. Jimmy gets injured in the group stages, and Alf sticks Geoff in, and well, the rest is glory.

That had to take courage. All of it. Imagine the manager now, the outcry on social media, the millions of us disagreeing with him, the pundits, the press, he'd be slaughtered . . .

Alf had a lot of doubters prior to the tournament. It was not a given that England would do well, let alone win it, despite his own confident declaration that we would. Plenty around the country weren't having that. England had never done well at a World Cup. Yes, we might be at home, but teams like the holders Brazil with Pelé, or the Germans, or the great Portuguese team with Eusébio, they were the ones to watch.

For us West Ham lads, there was an added reason for excitement. Four of our lot had made the provisional squad. Bobby, Geoff and Martin had been joined by Johnny Byrne, or 'Budgie' as we called him on account of his never shutting up. Budgie didn't make the cut but he was some striker and a great, great lad.

When Alf declared that, 'We will most certainly win the World Cup . . .' we all hoped that he would be right, of course we did, but it was hard to think they would go all the way. The squad was full of great players, but it was a young bunch. Geoff and Martin had only just got into the squad, Alan Ball was only twenty-one, and you would have been excused for thinking it was too soon for them.

Today, people like to talk about world class and debate who is and who isn't. That squad certainly had a few. Bobby Moore, of course, Bobby Charlton too. Gordon Banks in goal certainly was, and up front there was Greavsie, who certainly held that distinction. Bobby Moore and plenty of others would say Ray Wilson was, and he was very, very good. Arguably the best left-back in the world in 1966.

The game was changing. I was a winger and played against Ray, and he was strong and hard to beat, and with full-backs now getting on the move, crossing the halfway line, he was getting used to that side of the game. He would make a mistake in the final that led to the Germans' opening goal, but it was the rarest of errors from such a steady player. I know Bobby loved having him next to him at full-back.

At West Ham, we were managed by Ron Greenwood, the most forward-thinking and tactically astute coach around, and he must have been so proud of his players being in Alf's plans. They were all products of the club's youth policy, and we, having come through the same system, joined Ron with that sense of pride. Mind you, after the first group game, a goalless draw with Uruguay, we were probably pleased that two of them, Martin and Geoff, had been left out. It wasn't the best of performances and, after the game, all you could hear from people in the pub or out at the shops was, 'We ain't winning nothing!'

England won the next two group games. Two 2–0 wins over Mexico and then France were more than enough to see them progress but, still, there was no major expectation from the public, and those of us watching could see that Alf was still looking at his options. Alan Ball started that first game, as did Manchester Utd's John Connelly, but they were replaced with Southampton's Terry Paine and then Ian Callaghan, who helped his Liverpool teammate Roger Hunt to two goals against the French.

Roger is almost the forgotten striker in the 1966 story. So much is obviously made of Geoff replacing Greavsie, but Roger, who was clearly always in the manager's plans, was a fantastic goalscorer, and his three goals in the group stages proved vital. They came without much fanfare, but like all of them in '66, Roger, the most down to earth of Lancastrians, could not have cared less.

The bigger news from that win over France was that Greavsie had been hurt. Their midfielder, a bloke called Joseph Bonnel, a name that must have haunted Greavsie for the rest of his life, hit the England striker hard, scraping his studs down the shin and opening up the leg. It meant Jimmy needed fourteen stitches and was out for at least two games. You had to feel for him, the greatest finisher this country has ever produced. I played with Jimmy years later at West Ham, and that physical scar was very much visible.

My mate Geoff was going to get his chance, and he took it, along with Martin and Bally, who were picked in midfield. The quarter-final against Argentina was a tense one, niggly fouls everywhere, and when their number ten Antonio Rattín was sent off ten minutes before half-time, the Argentines dug in and made things very hard. I was at home with my parents, and watching the goal that settled it was like being at a West Ham training session. Martin Peters collects the ball out wide, draws the right-back, gets to the line and instinctively crosses the ball to the near post, where Geoff, well drilled by Ron in such matters, makes his run and nods it past the keeper.

It was a great moment. One that lifted the public from interested spectators to passionate citizens. Suddenly bunting was going up, people queuing in shops were talking about glorious possibilities, and blokes in pubs were discussing team selections. Of course, the topic of chat was whether Jimmy would get back in, but after a Bobby Charlton-inspired semi-final win over Eusébio's Portugal, there was no way Alf was going to change a winning team.

Jimmy knew that. Much has been said about his mood and how upset he was with Alf, but I don't think that was ever the case. Was he happy to miss the World Cup final? Of course not, but he was never moody around the players. He didn't go out on the night to celebrate the ultimate victory, but you can't blame him for that. Jimmy was only ever angry with the French player who did him, not the manager or his own teammates.

While we felt for Jimmy, there was a World Cup final to look forward to and, as ever, I would be watching it at home with my dad on our fairly new television. Not everyone had one, so you'd get neighbours and friends coming over, and I'd lapped up the whole tournament. I had been so excited to see Pelé but he fell victim to a more aggressive style of defending on show that summer, a trait making its way into the game.

Eusébio became the star but, as much as we loved him, we couldn't help but fall in love with the North Koreans who had knocked out the Italians in the group stages and now had the cheek to go 3–0 up against the mighty Portuguese in the quarters. The greatest shock of all time was on the cards until Eusébio had seen enough and led his lot to a 5–3 win.

The nation had really got into the competition, and with England in the final, it was all street parties and union flags everywhere. People hadn't seen anything like it since the queen's coronation thirteen years earlier. No one could wait for the final. It didn't cross my mind to make a phone call or two to my teammates about tickets. Mainly because we didn't have a phone! Anyway, I was more than happy to watch the game at home.

It was a special day. The streets were empty, pubs didn't show the games, and so everyone was in. At mine, we had a pot of tea on, some sandwiches, and it all got going. We're 1–0 down early on, but there's an equaliser, another West Ham goal, this time Mooro crossing for Geoff to head home, and then Martin scores with twelve minutes left and it looks like England have done it. Just seconds to go though, and it's heartbreak. The Germans grab a goal and it's extra-time. We're absolutely gutted.

What most impressed me about the team and their manager was how they lifted themselves up from the floor, literally in some cases, to go again and win the thing. That teamtalk before extra-time could have been very difficult. Alf himself must have been distraught. How close were

they? Seconds away from glory. It's got to be human nature to be thinking, as the clock is ticking down, about being a world champion. We all want to be professional, focus on the last moments, but those thoughts creep in, surely, and then, bang, a setpiece, a bit of a scramble in the box, and the ball is in the net. So close but sorry, another half hour. Gutted is the word.

But Alf brought all that energy to his teamtalk. I've watched. 'You've won it once, now win it again!' has to be one of the great rallying cries in the history of England. Shakespeare would have loved that one. 'Once more unto the breach . . .' has nothing on it.

And the players, for them, to have a little rub down, lift their spirits, and to go again, that takes a lot of doing. The occasion, the way the game has gone, the pressure of being hosts, they could have folded, but instead it's game faces back on, and out they go. 'Now win it again!'

I'm sure having a skipper like Bobby helped. Some people want all the chest-thumping, English bulldog stuff, and that has its place (it certainly did in the 1996 European Championship with Tony Adams). But I can imagine, being a player that day and seeing Bobby, his shorts and top still pristine, hardly a hair out of place, calmly just getting on with what had to be done . . . well, it must have made it easier for the lads to simply follow his example.

Geoff's goal to put England 3–2 up in extra-time has long been a controversial one and, even with today's

technology, it remains inconclusive, but I have always gone by Roger Hunt's reaction. Roger was an out-and-out goalscorer. A man obsessed with scoring, as his record shows. You don't remain Liverpool's all-time record league scorer for that long, and with the players they have had following him, without having a certain hunger to put the ball in the back of the net.

I met Roger a few times at Anfield, and as lovely and as humble as he was, I know that having followed up on Geoff's shot and seen it bounce, he would have thrown himself at it to score had he thought it never crossed the line. Yeah, that'll do me. It's a goal: 3–2, and England are leading again.

In my parents' living room, we were up and daring to believe again. The game ticked down, the Germans, their star young player Franz Beckenbauer unable to influence things (mainly because he was too keen on nullifying Bobby Charlton), were huffing and puffing a bit, but they were never going to stop, and they did launch forward for one last attack. The ball was floated into the England box, towards Mooro. I remember it like it was yesterday. The German attackers hovering, the penalty box is packed. Just head it out! That's what centre-halves do. Not Mooro. Bobby takes it on his chest and strolls to his left. 'Boot it!' we were shouting in our living room, and I imagine Alf was too. 'Just boot it, Bobby!'

Bobby isn't listening. Malcolm Allison's words about always looking to play from the back are probably ringing in his ears, so he plays a little one–two with Roger Hunt and bowls out with the ball towards the German forwards. 'Boot it!' He gets his head up and plays the most perfect forty-yard pass upfield, and Geoff does the rest, grabbing his hat-trick and winning England the World Cup.

It was the best moment. It was crazy to think my mates were on that pitch and had achieved what they had. We were all up and embracing in the front room, and then I settled down, another cup of tea on the go, and a big smile on my face watching all the lads taking their applause. The three West Ham boys sure, but to see Nobby Stiles skipping about, Bobby Charlton and his brother Jack, two very different men but in an emotional sibling embrace, it was magic.

Alan Ball too. Alan had been man-of-the-match, a performance of never-ending energy and enthusiasm that summed up the player and the bloke. I loved Bally. He never changed. Always bubbly, always great company, Bally was some player. His game was based upon that energetic nature, but what a footballer too. Some players excel at playing one-touch football, Bally could play half-touch. He was so deft, two-footed, so clever.

He would tell me about growing up in the north-west, and how much he practised. Kicking a ball, all day, again and again, left foot, right foot, again and again. No wonder he was so comfortable with it at his feet. He had trials with lots of clubs, but his diminutive stature put some off. One manager told him to try being a jockey instead, but Bally persevered and in the end Blackpool took him on. Bally ran home (always running) and skipped into his house to tell his dad the news.

'Dad, Dad, they want to sign me, they want to sign me, I've made it.'

Bally's dad looked up from his paper and said, 'You ain't made nothing, son, now get into the garden and practise.'

What I enjoyed most was knowing just how much they loved the game and how much they just adored playing it. I'm not saying modern players don't, of course they do, but there is so much that goes with being a pro these days, all the social media, the contracts, the possibility for transfers and change. That wasn't around back then. These players played that World Cup final with that same enthusiasm the likes of Bally showed as a kid practising. Yes, there was glory but it was all about playing football, that was the big buzz.

At West Ham, during the summer, we'd all meet up and play. Young players, senior pros, anyone who hadn't taken the family down to the beach. The season would be over, but on a Tuesday or a Thursday we'd meet up and play. On Sunday mornings, we'd met over at Hainault golf course, where there was a nice flat bit of grass, and we'd play. Sometimes fourteen-a-side games, but we'd play.

A few of our pals would join in. Myself, Frank Lampard Snr, Johnny Charles, Bobby Moore, everyone and anyone who was about.

We couldn't get enough, we were happiest playing, we loved being in each other's company, and that team, on that famous afternoon at the old Wembley Stadium, was no different. They'd done it, they'd done it together, and while, in my opinion, they were all treated pretty shabbily by the FA and the establishment as a whole, they remained the best of men.

Having had a night out, albeit stuck out by the toilets at Danny La Rue's, Bobby went home, and two weeks later, he was back for pre-season training, as if nothing had happened. No airs or graces, but none of them had. No asking for more time off, no going on about it, no medals on show. We might have bought them an extra pint in the Black Lion. But that would have been it. That's probably all they wanted.

It's still there: what that bunch of blokes did that summer is still very much part of all of us. As an England player, you felt it. Not as a hindrance, but as an aspiration and an inspiration. It was always there, the bar was set, and us future generations have to try to reach up and match it. The song talks about our thirty years of pain, but that's now sixty years, and that team still hasn't been matched: 1966 is still the benchmark.

We, as pundits and fans, still reference it. During the 2024 Euros, Harry Kane doesn't look fit, he's England's star striker, a goalscoring talisman, but he's not himself. To some, he needs to be dropped. To others, the suggestion is absolute nuts, but invariably the argument lands on 1966 and the fact that Alf was ballsy enough to leave out his star player.

I remember watching the 2022 World Cup final. Kylian Mbappé gets his hat-trick, it's an incredible game, France end up losing but he is rightly lauded as the best striker in the world. However, our minds turn to Geoff, West Ham's Geoff Hurst, and what he did on 30 July 1966. Header, right-foot, and left-foot. And he won the game. Beat that.

Chapter 3

The Gaffers

HARRY

I played for and came up against some of the truly great managers of the English game, but the first one that deserves a mention is a fantastic bloke called Albert Chamberlain. Albert lived on the same Burdett Estate in Poplar as my parents and me, and as a boy, he was the first man to start a local kids' football team, the first man to pick me to play in it, and so I guess he was the first man I thought of as the boss.

My dad had, of course, instilled that love of football in me, and when he moved us to the estate, it was like heaven. Suddenly there were loads of kids to play the game with, and we spent every spare hour out on some part of the flats, kicking a ball around.

We even had a small but flat patch of grass that we nicknamed 'Wembley'. That was the ultimate, and a game in the summer out on its hallowed turf could last all day. During the school year, you'd get home, drop your bag, but having already heard from some other kid on your way in that there was, 'a game on at Wembley', your mum wouldn't see you for long because you were straight back out to join in.

FA Cup final day, the only televised game of the year, that was spent, obviously, in front of the telly, any telly you could find. After the match, it was straight out on to our version of the famous stadium to recreate the two teams and try to score a goal like Villa's Peter McParland or Manchester Utd's Tommy Taylor in the 1957 final. Games would go on into the night, only broken up a bit by the shrill of mums all over the estate shouting us boys in for something to eat. 'Peter! Dinner!' you'd hear. 'Terry! Get in now, your dinner's ready!'

If it wasn't our mums disrupting our cup finals with matters of grub, it was the estate caretaker. A horrible little man, who for some reason didn't like us lads playing. There were no cars on the estate so we had freedom to play, and our parents were certainly pleased to know we were kicking a ball rather than smashing windows, but for some reason this man took offence at us.

He would try to sneak up on us, and as he was only about four feet two, that was easier than it sounds. We'd always be on to him, though, before he could nick the ball. One day as he chased us off, Albert Chamberlain strolled around the corner and wondered what was going on. Albert had another football-mad boy on the estate, a kid called Alan, and when he saw us all running, he was having none of it.

If the caretaker was a very small man, Albert was a very big one. Like my old man, he was a docker, and he was hard as nails. Lovely but very tough looking. 'What's going on?' Albert asked. The caretaker sheepishly told him that we were causing aggro, and that he was going to report us to our mums.

'Oh why don't you leave them alone?' Albert said. 'Ain't you got nothin' better to do? Go on, sod off, what harm are they doin'?'

The caretaker never bothered us after that, but for Albert it planted an idea in his head, and seeing how much his boy and all of us loved playing, he soon came up with a plan. 'We're gonna start our own team.' We all loved the idea immediately. 'We'll call ourselves Burdett Boys.'

With that a team was born, and Albert took it very seriously. He got us a kit, and he found us an under-11s league. It was a bit of a way away over on Regent's Park but it was an organised league and, even though as a bunch of nine- and eight-year-olds we were playing against older lads and getting chinned most weeks, we absolutely loved it.

On a Friday after school, we'd all meet in a tiny unused room that we called the Matchbox. None of us knew what it was for, but we would get in there, and Albert would go over tactics for the game on the Sunday morning. It was the first boot room of sorts that I ever went in. In time, Albert got to know more and more kids in the area, and nicked them to play for us. It wasn't long before we had two teams, moved to a more local league over on the Hackney Marshes, and Burdett Boys, serial title-winners, became one of the best and most respected kids' teams in east London. It was all down to the boss, Albert Chamberlain.

Not that we stopped playing our games on the estate, and even in the winter months we could play late because there was a small light by the old pram sheds.

By now, I had been doing some training with Tottenham, even meeting one of the great managers, Bill Nicholson, who told me he'd heard I was doing OK out on the wing, but wondered if I scored goals.

'No, Mr Nicholson,' I said a bit sheepishly. 'I don't score many goals.'

Bill frowned.

'Well, I only know one great winger who never scored many goals, and his name was Stanley Matthews. Unless you're going to be as good as him, you'd better start scoring.'

I'd train twice a week with Tottenham, the best team in the country at the time, but you'd still find me most other nights playing under the one little light by those pram sheds. One evening, in the darkness, we noticed two men watching us, too tall to be the dreaded caretaker. And as they eventually stepped out into the light, I saw that one of them was Tommy Docherty, by now the young manager at Chelsea.

The Doc had brought his chief scout with him, a guy called Wilf Chitty, and together they asked if they could talk to me and my dad about going over there to train instead. It was nice to be wanted but, as we sat in my living room, I think my dad was more excited about meeting Tommy than he was in my immediate future. Tommy had been a hero of my old man in his recent playing days at Arsenal, and over several cups of tea, they talked and talked about football and those good old days.

I really liked Tommy, and I liked the idea of Chelsea as I knew they put a lot of faith in young players. Soon, with the likes of Allan and Ron Harris, Eddie McCreadie and Terry Venables, they would become affectionately known as 'Docherty's Diamonds'. As much as I was flattered by Tommy coming to see me on the estate and as excited as my dad was to have him around for tea, by now my head had been turned by West Ham.

Arsenal had come in too, but they had a reputation for buying talent rather than nurturing it, and so it really came down to the manager at Upton Park. Every time I went to a youth game, Ron Greenwood was there – not now and then, like others, but every time, and he wasn't there as a gesture. It was clear that he cared, and that he genuinely saw the lads in the youth team as very much his and his team's future.

My best pal at the time, Colin Mackleworth, the goalkeeper at Burdett Boys, was going to West Ham, which might have had some influence on my decision, but ultimately it was Ron's presence that made up my mind.

Ron was the most forward-thinking manager in the country. His methods, his faith in youth, his ability to make players better . . . it was everything a young footballer would want. He also understood that us young lads, despite now being with a professional club, were not going to change, and that deep down we were still those same boys from our various estates.

At just fifteen, on our way to winning the 1963 Youth Cup final but still apprentices, we would look for ways – once we'd finished all our jobs around the ground – to have a game. At Upton Park there was a car park so we'd get over there, find a good clear spot and we'd have a bit of a game. It could go on quite late and one of the club's trainers, a legend called Ernie Gregory, a former keeper at West Ham, would clock us and shout over, 'Pack it in, lads. It's half past four. Ain't you got homes to get to?'

Ernie might have been far from as annoying as the old caretaker on the Burdett Estate, but he was spoiling our fun. We needn't have worried because when Ron

Greenwood found out that our impromptu games were being stopped, he intervened. He got hold of Ernie and said that if we wanted to stay and play, we could, and that as long as we were playing football, we could stay as long as we wanted. He even arranged for adults to be there to make sure we all got home safe.

Like Albert Chamberlain, he was a manager who just wanted us lads to play.

JAMIE

One of my first managers, unlike Albert Chamberlain or Ron Greenwood, actually worried that I was playing too much. I played above my age group, and I played on a Saturday morning, and then again on Saturday afternoon. One guy coaching me showed a bit of concern, arguing that you have to be very careful with young players and watch out for injuries. Dad, being old-school, wasn't having that. 'Just play!' He probably had Albert and Ron's words in his head, and I certainly wasn't going to argue. He saw how much I loved it. One game would finish, lovely, little break, something to eat, and off we go again. Looking back, retiring at thirty-one and getting a knee replacement at fifty, maybe that guy was right! Maybe he knew more than my dad!

To be fair, I've not met many people who do know more about the game than my dad, and it was a pleasure and

an education to be around him and his football teams, initially as his boy at his knee, following him everywhere around the training ground (or the local park as it was back then) and then as a young pro at Bournemouth, as a midfielder keen to learn more.

With that education, when someone like Kenny Dalglish became interested when I was just seventeen and was willing to pay £350,000, going up to around half-a-million quid (making me the most expensive teenager in football – no pressure then!), we were going to listen. Dad probably wanted the money for a new kitchen for Mum!

Kenny was a legend. A bona fide legend of the global game, right up there in the argument about Britain's best players, but he is also one of our greatest people and, having spent time with him, there could be no doubt that going to Liverpool was the right move for me. Kenny didn't have to sell the club in any way, it spoke for itself, but I knew that this was a manager and a man that I would run through walls for. I still would.

What I didn't know, at the time, was that Kenny was going through his own personal hell. He had done so much for the people of Liverpool, taking on so much to help those who had lost loved ones at the Hillsborough disaster in April 1989, just some eighteen months before. That, coupled with the pressures that come with managing the biggest club in the country, took its toll. Just over a month after I signed, Kenny resigned.

It was a massive moment. Kenny *was* Liverpool Football Club. As a manager he had won three titles, one as a player-manager (he was still the best player in training when I arrived, by the way), and just seemed to be a permanent part of the club he had helped make great. But, and we can forget this about our sporting greats, he was also just human, and had to look out for himself and his family.

I remember hearing the news. It was a Friday and, in training, Ronnie Moran (stepping in as caretaker manager) told me I wouldn't be travelling with the squad for the game at Luton the following day. He explained that the club was under siege a bit, and they wanted to take only senior players. It might have made sense, but I was gutted.

I was in shock. The man who had signed me, the man who had shown so much faith in me, had gone. I headed back to the digs I was living in. I remember getting to the door, stopping and bursting into tears. The manager I longed to play for had gone and now I would never get the chance.

I was distraught. I took myself up to my room, and the phone rang downstairs.

'Jamie, it's for you.'

I presumed it was my mum or dad checking in on me, but to my surprise it was Kenny. Kenny, on the day of his big announcement, and no doubt being inundated with calls from a frenzied press, had taken the time to call me to explain his reasons, to say that he knew I was very much the future of the football club, and that he was playing nine holes of golf the next day and he'd love me to join him. It was an incredible gesture from an incredible man.

I only had five weeks with Kenny as a manager, but his permanent replacement was another Liverpool great. Graeme Souness was a force of nature and I am still very fond of him. It didn't go great for him at Liverpool, and some will say he tried too much, too soon, but I learned loads from him, and having played out in Italy, he certainly tried to take the club into more modern times.

He could be fierce, though. Charming and engaging but with a spark that you knew was ready to go off at any time. I remember, I was eighteen, I had played loads under Graeme, but he had left me out for a couple of games. Now, with the wisdom of age, I know that he was resting me, trying not to overplay the younger players, but then I was a bit annoyed. No agents, remember, so I called my dad.

'Why aren't I playing?'

Dad told me that there was nothing wrong with knocking on the manager's door and asking the question. He said that he preferred a player doing that to sulking and that the following morning I should march up to the door, give it a good knock, confidently walk in, and request some answers.

'OK, Dad.'

I didn't sleep very well that night. This was Graeme Souness. Walk confidently? Knock loudly? Demand answers? How was that going to go?

The next day, I'm at the door, I give it a tap, walk in with a far from purposeful stride, and I say, 'Hi, boss, all good, I hope I can play soon.'

'You will.'

'Nice one, thanks, see you later.'

It wasn't the big scene Dad might have envisaged, but I guess I got my answer!

Managers don't mind players getting a bit upset about not playing. I didn't. I wanted them to show a bit of character, come and ask some questions. Nothing aggressive, but a good knock on the door, and a chat about my reasons, and what they might do to improve a bit. That is all perfectly fine.

In my time, it was much more about relationships between players and staff. Maybe that's gone a bit, I don't know, but in my latter years, I could see that there was less knocking on managers' doors and more texting. At Tottenham, I named a team once, and one player, unhappy that he wasn't starting, sat, said nothing, didn't look at me, and began to write a text. I later found out that he was messaging his agent, and his agent would, in turn, soon be messaging the chairman.

Why not talk to me, even if it's to scream and shout? Ask me why and then get your head down and work even harder. That's what Frank Lampard Snr did when he was a young footballer at West Ham. Ron Greenwood saw that, in Frank, he had a brilliant player, tenacious and with a great left foot, but he couldn't run. It was a problem, and Ron suggested that he go and get some game time at Torquay.

Loads of the West Ham boys went to play down in Devon with Torquay, on loan or sold. The two clubs had a connection, but the thing is, Frank wasn't having any of it. 'I'm not going,' he said to Ron. Ron was clever enough to know that Frank meant it, and without a big fuss he let him get on with things. Frank went away, got some running spikes, and he worked. He worked every day. Out there, sprinting, short little bursts, and in time he went from the slowest in the squad to more than fast enough, and won a couple of international caps.

His son, Frank Jnr, was just the same. Frank had all the talent, he could play, but like his dad, he needed to work on his mobility. Every single day he'd be out there after training, running but also working on shooting. A bag of balls on his own, sprinting and shooting, over and over. Some players might have been a bit snide about it, thinking that he was overdoing it, but when younger teammates like Joe Cole and Rio Ferdinand saw how his work was paying off, they did the same.

Managers dream of having pros like that.

Today, players who are dropped might still text their agents, but their agents are also immediately – sometimes before the game has even kicked off – posting on social media wondering why their guy has been left out. It just underlines how difficult a manager's job has become in modern times.

Actually, it probably always was a tough job. It's just that when I was growing up, watching from the outside, the managers seemed, not always calm, but quietly in control. Bob Paisley at Liverpool, Bobby Robson at Ipswich, Ron Greenwood, Dad's old boss and manager of England. They had a way about them, footballing men, in the business of coaching and letting the players do the talking.

They all had that look. My dad had it. Alex Ferguson had it. The suit and tie, maybe a mackintosh on a rainy or windy day. They looked like headmasters. It was a uniform they wore, a show of their hushed authority. Dad was superstitious, though. If his team were winning he would wear the same suit and tie until they lost.

Things have changed a bit now, and managers are cool. Pep Guardiola might wear the cargo pants, and Jürgen Klopp somehow managed to make the full tracksuit plus some merch from the club shop look good. More and more managers these days are *the* big deal, but back then, while they would have been everything to their football clubs when I was young, it all seemed to be done with the minimum of fuss and personality.

And then along came Brian Clough. I would have had no problem playing with a manager like Clough. I've asked Roy Keane about him in the past, Stuart Pearce too, as they both played under Clough at Nottingham Forest, and it was about making the players feel like they were the best around. To be around a personality like Clough, in his prime, must have lifted the players and every day must have been different. Unfortunately, I do think it was his outspoken personality that cost him (and the country) the chance to manage the national team. It would have been incredible to have him at the helm, but I think the Football Association has always shied away from people like Brian, managers that speak their mind, and manage in their own distinct way.

When the England job came up in the early 1980s, Clough had just taken Nottingham Forest from the Second Division to the First Division title and won the European Cup in successive seasons. Imagine not getting the England job on the back of that? To not choose him was all about his personality and that seems a great waste. We lost a box-office manager and I don't think England have had one before or since.

Managers just weren't high profile when I was growing up. Matt Busby was a great man and, after Munich, everyone in the whole country wanted him to do well (especially in the European Cup), whoever they supported, but he was still quietly on the sidelines, and when Manchester United came locally to play, it was all about seeing the great players he had assembled.

Liverpool's Bill Shankly was arguably the first real, big personality in the dugout. Not many have matched the great man for personality since, to be fair. I got hold of Shankly's interviews on tape, and when I was a young manager, driving all over the country, I'd stick these tapes on in the car and listen to him, taking inspiration from everything he said, and how he said it. Players must have run out of his dressing room feeling like a million dollars. Bill was fantastic.

My first trip away with the West Ham first team was up to Anfield. Bill had built his first great team: Ian Callaghan, Roger Hunt, Ian St John, Ron Yeats, wonderful footballers. When we got there, though, Bill had no interest in his lot: he was just stood at the players' entrance, waiting for our bus to arrive, and as we walked off he eyed us up and down. He then went off to tell his lot that we looked terrified or had been on the lash the night before.

I heard a story years later that when a young Kevin Keegan was starting out, Liverpool came to us at West Ham. Bill had had given us his once over, and went into his dressing room, sat next to young Kevin and told him that Bobby Moore had bags under his eyes, that there was dandruff on his lapels and that he had clearly been out on the town. Keegan, perhaps aided by Bill's demystification of the great Mooro, played well and Liverpool won 2–1. After the game, Bill said to his young striker, 'You'll never play against anyone better than him.'

Shanks and Sir Matt were the big names in management in the 1960s, and up in Scotland, there was Jock Stein, very underrated and making history with Celtic. All three men were from mining communities in Scotland, and all three went down the pits. It must have affected their approach to management. Look at Sir Alex Ferguson: he was from a shipbuilding community in Govan in Glasgow, where similar work ethics were instilled in him.

My own dad was a docker, and while I am not saying I am in the same category as those greats, it does say something about the backgrounds of the men who used to be managers. Some, if not most, were not interested in making headlines. That's why it was so incredible when along came Cloughie, this force of nature, able to talk as much as Muhammad Ali.

Cloughie was incredible, but he was as shrewd as they come. Signing Dave Mackay from Spurs in 1968, when he was at Derby, was a masterstroke. Some thought that Dave was finished, but Cloughie took him to the Baseball Ground, and the great man helped them to promotion and won the Football Writer's Player of the Year.

It was a brilliant bit of out-of-the-box thinking. I certainly took inspiration from it when I took Paul Merson to Portsmouth in 2002. A player who some might think was looking back on his best days, but able to bring so much quality and ultimately success to our group.

Cloughie actually blocked a signing I was trying to make in 1990. One that I had high hopes for. At Bournemouth, we had heard good things about a talented left-footed lad playing non-league at Runcorn, called Ian Woan. Myself and my scout, Stewart Morgan, went up to the north-west on a freezing night, were very impressed, and sorted out a fee for £40,000. We arranged for Ian and his dad to get down to Bournemouth to sign a couple of days later. It never happened. He signed for Nottingham Forest.

I later found out from a pal, Alan Hill, one of Cloughie's assistants, that one afternoon they were sitting around after training, and on the old news service, Teletext, it came up that Bournemouth were close to finalising the transfer.

Brian took a look at the screen. 'That Redknapp does well with non-league players,' he said to his staff. 'Who is this fella Woan?'

Another member of Cloughie's staff, Ronnie Fenton, knew the manager at Runcorn and made a phone call. 'Is this Woan any good?' he asked.

'He's too good for bloody Bournemouth,' came the reply.

Forest made a bid of £80,000 and the deal was done.

Away from transfers, Cloughie's genius lay in how he got the best out of his players, and sometimes that meant a bit of manipulation. I hired Jim Smith to work with me at Portsmouth, knowing that he could often play the bad cop to my good. It was a trick Cloughie had down to a tee.

If a player looked unfit, Brian would get his assistant Ronnie to take them to the stands, and have them running up and down the steps. Eventually Brian would come out from the tunnel and shout, 'Oi Ronnie, what the hell are you doing with the poor lad?' The guy would stop, and Cloughie would be all smiles and say, 'Come on, let's get the ball out and have some fun.'

The player had done his sprints, and Brian was the good guy.

When I was young, I had a keen interest in Italian football. I supported Juventus but, later in the 1980s, it was AC Milan and Arrigo Sacchi's incredible team that grabbed everyone's attention. I got that Sacchi was a great manager, but the focus was on the players. Ruud Gullit, Marco van Basten, Roberto Donadoni were incredible talent, but what I didn't appreciate was that Sacchi's methods and tactics were not only bringing the very best from the players but changing and influencing football forever. Johan Cruyff was doing the same in Spain.

The way they went about building teams, playing with intensity, changing training methods, it had an effect on the coaches that followed them and the likes of Pep Guardiola and Jürgen Klopp would take what these

pioneers did and use it to give us in England two of the most talked-about teams of modern times.

Our greatest manager is arguably Sir Alex Ferguson. I came up against his formidable sides, and while you can't say he drastically changed the game like Sacchi or Cruyff, the environment that he created over so many years and the unending success that he brought to Manchester United was just unbelievable. I won't lie, it could make you a bit jealous, because as good a team as we had at Liverpool and as good as the managers were that I played under there, whatever we did, we just couldn't topple them, and it all seemed to stem from the manager.

His achievements at Aberdeen prior to coming to England were great enough, but to build Manchester United up in the way he did, it took a talent very rarely seen. It also took a bit of luck and a bit of time, and any manager will tell you that they need both. Luck may be rare but today time is non-existent. Make no mistake, in the modern era, Fergie would have been sacked at Old Trafford before he brought success.

Instead he got some time, and after four years won the FA Cup in 1990, built upon that, won another cup, blooded an incredible group of young players in the mid-1990s, and then, with the success that he unerringly achieved, he set about adding to his squads with the best players. Need a defender? Rio Ferdinand is the best in the country. Need goals? Andy Cole is the top scorer.

Years later, so was Wayne Rooney. Layer upon layer of brilliant decisions. It's hard to see a manager being at a club as long as Ferguson was at Old Trafford, and he is, of course, lauded by many as the greatest to have managed in this country. It's an argument that fans of Bob Paisley would want a say in, and I personally think Pep's achievements, not only in winning what he has, but also in how he so drastically changed football, make him a strong candidate. We're talking the true greats in the history of management, but I would go with Pep.

It's hard to see past Sir Alex. If anything, his longevity alone is a remarkable achievement, especially in the more modern era where time is something managers used to crave, but is now a luxury most know they'll never have. Instant success is what it is all about.

Speaking of success, I used to have a bit against Alex. I lost more than I won of course (who didn't?), but there were some notable wins, especially in the FA Cup. I got on great with Alex. I tried to get on with all the managers I faced, but certainly would never show reverence towards any of them, and that included the Manchester United man. We did, however, have a bit in common, and when we travelled to Old Trafford, in those dead minutes after the players have gone out for their warm-up and as the nerves start to jangle, Alex would be there. 'Coming in for a cup of tea, Harry?' he'd say. In his office, with the horses on the television, a well-thumbed copy of the *Racing Post* on the desk, we'd chat about the day's bets, maybe a good player we'd heard about in League Two, or how our sons were doing. It was always the hardest away game at Old Trafford, but there wasn't one at which I was made to feel more welcome or relaxed.

After the game, there was a nice glass of wine and a fond farewell. I did win there a couple of times, knocking United out of the Cup with both West Ham and Portsmouth. It's funny because, on those occasions, that glass of wine was half empty, and the farewell a little bit less fond. Like all great competitors, Sir Alex Ferguson was a very sore loser.

One man who might have seen that more than most was Arsène Wenger, who came in at Arsenal in 1996 and put a cat among Fergie's pigeons. No one knew much about the Frenchman, but in he came and built a couple of teams that rank high in the English game's history books.

I say built, but Arsène would be the first to say that he had a tremendous amount of luck when he arrived. Good fortune is as vital to a manager as his coaches and players, and to walk into a dressing room that included a defence like Arsenal's is the biggest blessing any manager has ever had.

Having Tony Adams alone would be great but with David Seaman, Lee Dixon, Nigel Winterburn, Steve Bould and Martin Keown there too? Bloody hell. And that's just the defence. Bruce Rioch, his predecessor, had bought Dennis Bergkamp. Thanks for that, Bruce! I'm not saying that Arsène had it easy, not at all, none of us do, but what he did have was a foundation, and on top of that he could bring his fantastic knowledge of the French and African markets and build his title-winning teams.

I got on with Arsène; we never had any problems, even when we were north London rivals, but he was different from Ferguson. There was no tea and chat before a game, and I hardly ever saw him afterwards. He wasn't at other games scouting, and he wasn't at youth games either, but that became more and more normal in the game towards the end. Methods were changing and so was the job.

When I was at Liverpool, a few managers tried to get Alex Ferguson's wine glass to be half empty, but it wasn't always easy. Under Roy Evans, we had a good go and we had good results against Manchester United, but we just couldn't find that consistency to push them all the way to a title.

Kenny Dalglish was actually the first to upset Fergie's Premier League applecart. He is rightly regarded as one of our greatest footballers, but what a managerial career too, by the way. After he won those three titles at Liverpool, he won the Premier League at Blackburn in 1995. Some say the latter was due to Jack Walker's wealth, but plenty of teams spent money and failed. Kenny was so clever, he got Ray Harford in with him, who was a great footballing man, and then what Kenny had was a great eye for players.

It didn't take a genius to see that Alan Shearer was a goal machine, but he added Chris Sutton to play off him, Tim Sherwood to be the legs in midfield, Graeme Le Saux, Stuart Ripley, Jason Wilcox and Colin Hendry. He also inherited and used players like Mark Atkins, not the biggest name but a midfielder who Sherwood always used to tell me was a dream to play with. Great pros, the lot of them. Like Fergie, Kenny could buy the best, but he did it cleverly: he didn't just splatter-gun the squad with big names, he pieced together a great team and a great squad.

I almost spoiled their party. When they came to Anfield on the last day of the 1994–5 season, needing either to win or for Manchester United to not win at Dad's West Ham, I scored a last-minute free-kick past Tim Flowers. I remember my reaction. I genuinely thought, 'Oh fuck, I'm going to upset Kenny.' It wasn't about wanting Manchester United to fail, or about Liverpool, my thoughts were quickly all about Kenny. My hand went on my head, and I am thinking, 'What have I done?'

After the game, with Blackburn lifting the trophy at our place, Kenny came up to me with a smile. 'What were you thinking, Jamie?' I didn't really have an answer. West Ham had got a draw against Manchester United, though, so at least one of us Redknapps behaved that day.

At Liverpool, we were desperate to achieve the same thing as Blackburn, but it wasn't to be. Roy Evans got us close. Roy was great with me, and a great football man. He had grown up in the Anfield boot room and brought all that experience with him into the job. Football was moving on, yes, and old beer crates for chairs and men drinking bottles of stout while talking football might have sounded antiquated, but that's not what Roy was all about. He was a modern coach. Roy's adoption of a 3–5–2 system was laughed at by some, but it worked brilliantly for us; it got the best out of our best players like Steve McManaman, brought us a lot of joy, and plenty of teams have followed since.

When we, as a group, were tagged as 'The Spice Boys', many saw that as a slight on Roy and his discipline. Roy was a gentleman, a nice guy, but do not think for one minute that us players took advantage. We were young and we went out, but so did everyone. The spotlight was on us instead of Manchester United (who very much liked a night out too) because they were winning trophies and we weren't. We worked so hard in training, pushed by competitive pros like John Barnes and Ian Rush, and Roy, with Ronnie Moran by his side, was never going to go easy on us.

We got stick for losing, that's OK, part of the job, but we were up against Ferguson's United and in the end they were better than us. That doesn't belittle Roy's efforts or the team's. Fergie had great players – Roy Keane and the Class of '92 (Beckham, Giggs, Scholes, Butt and the Nevilles), they were brilliant – but that shouldn't be a stick to beat Roy Evans or us with. Yes, you can always do more. With hindsight we can say maybe Roy should have brought in that player or not signed certain individuals, but they are minute details.

After Roy, Gérard Houllier certainly brought success and trophies back to Anfield, and on a personal note, I owed him everything for, in 1999, giving me the captaincy, and I could never thank him enough for that honour. To lead the team out of the tunnel and turn right towards the Kop with that armband on was the most special moment, and along with putting on an England shirt, the most memorable of my career.

Gérard was a new breed of football manager. A former schoolteacher, he had no playing career to talk of. Arsène Wenger played more than Gérard but still, these were new thinkers in the game, able to draw on their knowledge of football rather than their experience in it. One guy who had no background in football but who blew the English game wide open was José Mourinho.

Gérard Houllier never played at any sort of high level but he came with a big background in setting up new methods with the French national team, but when José arrived on the scene, a former translator now winning the Champions League with Porto in 2004, it just blew up and he felt like a trailblazer.

How can a guy come into our game, having not played the game, and be so confident, be so sure of himself? I wasn't sure about him at first. Maybe simply because we'd not seen anyone like him before. What he did in the English game was unbelievable, though. Those Chelsea teams he built were among the very best.

Yes, he has given me a bit of stick as a pundit, and I have returned it. If I have, it's because I was a player, and I just sometimes felt that he was taking all the credit for a team's success. I wanted the players to get the praise (my cousin Frank Lampard Jnr was one of them, after all), but that was that, I was being a pundit, that's the job. At the end of it all, though, I have nothing but respect for him. José was great for the game, and he had a great eye for it, you can't deny that.

He was brilliant with the mind games, one of the best, and more than able to take on Ferguson at his own game. With Fergie and Wenger and then José, needle became part of the Premier League and its coverage for a while, but it seems to have dropped out of it, for now. We're human beings and so maybe we miss the theatre of all of that, but the more modern rivalries, such as that between Pep Guardiola and Jürgen Klopp, have been about the game and the players, and two very different styles and personalities.

You might like Jürgen's high-octane, so-called 'heavy metal' approach, or you might like Pep's clinical and technical style of football. There's no right answer, but what the public got were some of the great games in the Premier League era and the couple of seasons that saw both teams rack up points in the nineties will be hard to beat for sheer excellence.

I personally have nothing but respect for managers. I thought about doing it, but having seen the intense pressure my dad was put under – from a young age, even at school in Bournemouth I'd hear kids moaning about him if the side had lost – I quickly knew it wasn't for me. I sometimes look at Frank Jnr and wonder if he chose to go into it because his dad wasn't under that same scrutiny, but now with social media on top of the constant phone-ins, I think I made the right choice. Having said all that, I will never stop respecting the gaffers.

I often get asked if being a manager is harder today than it was back in my day. It's hard to say either way, but what I don't envy about the modern game is the constant scrutiny. I thought I had it bad when there was one radio phone-in, and I got constant stick from that former Conservative MP, David Mellor, who presented it. That was grating enough, but today, with all the different podcasts and social media platforms, it's never ending.

There is also the changing face of technology within the management game. When I started out at Bournemouth, technology in the dressing room meant a new screw to replace your studs. When I was at Portsmouth in the 2000s, it became more and more usual to have things like Prozone software to aid the coaches, and we did take a young Michael Edwards on there, who knew loads about it. Michael has gone on to do amazing things at Liverpool, but I would be lying if I said I wasn't a bit baffled by all the new fads.

I came from the generation that spent time on the road, going to matches, getting tip-offs about players, watching them, making decisions based on gut instinct rather than data. I'm not wanting to sound like an old fuddy-duddy, and I appreciate what technology can do for the modern coach; it's just that I feel sad that managers today only work on the here and now. There is no nurturing of the club or the young players, because there simply is no time. They have to win now, so who cares about the future?

When I was managing, my Saturday mornings were spent at the youth-team games. I had taken Ron Greenwood's example of caring for the young players as if they were the seniors, and that meant being over the training ground every week, without fail, and then heading off to the ground for the first-team game. I go to plenty of youth football these days, and I have never seen a first-team manager at any of them. That's a real shame.

As well as investing in my youth teams, when I was managing I never forgot my elders either. When I became the boss at West Ham, there was an older gentleman who

Harry: It was a full house the day I went with my dad to watch Manchester United play at Arsenal in February 1958. Little did anyone know that it would be the last game that the 'Busby Babes' played on English soil prior to the Munich air disaster.
(Photo by Reg Burkett/Keystone/Hulton Archive/Getty Images)

Harry: To many, including my dad, Sir Tom Finney was the best post-war footballer. Even the great Manchester City goalkeeper, Bert Trautmann can't stop him (No. 9 on the floor) scoring for Preston North End in 1959. *(Colorsport/Shutterstock)*

Harry: England's greatest ever footballer? It's hard to see past the great Sir Bobby Charlton. Here he is taking on the French during a World Cup group game at Wembley in July 1966.
(Trinity Mirror/Mirropix/Alamy Stock Photo)

Jamie: 'Uncle Bobby!' It was rare to see mud on Moore's shorts but here he is seeing off the Germans during the 1966 World Cup final.
(Photo by Popperfoto via Getty Images)

Harry: That's miles over the line! Geoff Hurst' second and England's third goal in the 1966 World Cup final. We've always thought that Roger Hunt's (arms outstretched) reaction confirmed that the ball crossed the line.
(Associated Press/Alamy Stock Photo)

Harry: Still the pinnacle. The 1966 World Cup winning squad was full of great lads, and Bobby Moore was their perfect captain.
(Photo by Evening Standard/Hulton Archive/Getty Images)

Harry: The picture on my wall. There was nothing but mutual respect between Pelé and Bobby Moore, as shown in this iconic photo taken after Brazil's 1–0 win over England at the 1970 World Cup. *(Photo by MSI/Mirrorpix via Getty Images)*

Harry: There's no stopping the great Brazilian midfielder Gérson's strike that put Brazil 2–1 up against Italy in the 1970 World Cup final. *(Photo by Popperfoto via Getty Images/Getty Images)*

Harry: The captain Carlos Alberto celebrates scoring Brazil's magnificent fourth in their 4–1 win over Italy in the 1970 World Cup final. Has there ever been a better team goal? *(Photo by Popperfoto via Getty Images/Getty Images)*

Harry: I beat my full back playing for West Ham at Upton Park in March 1967.
(Photo by Ed Lacey/Popperfoto via Getty Images)

Harry: Jamie (left) and his brother Mark show off their American fashion sense at a match in the States in the late '70s.

Jamie: We were so lucky to have Bobby Moore in our lives. Here is the great man with me when we were all living and playing in the United States.

(above) Harry: A family day out. I took both Jamie and his brother to see West Ham beat Arsenal 1–0 in the 1980 FA Cup final at Wembley. Jamie's uncle Frank Lampard Sr. tussles with Arsenal's Liam Brady. *(Photo by Evening Standard/ Getty Images)*

(right) **Jamie: Pitting my wits against my cousin Frank Lampard in a game between Southampton and Chelsea in April 2005.** *(Back Page Images/ Shutterstock)*

Jamie: The Brazilian, who sparked my imagination, takes on England's Trevor Brooking in an international played in Los Angeles in 1976. *(Photo by Popperfoto via Getty Images/Getty Images)*

Harry: One of the greatest matches of all time. Marco Tardelli (right) was a fantastic player, but the Italian's 3–2 victory over Brazil at the 1982 World Cup broke a lot of hearts (including Jamie's). *(Photo by Bob Thomas Sports Photography via Getty Images)*

Harry: Italy had kicked Diego Maradona to pieces four years earlier in Spain, but there was no stopping the little genius at the 1986 World Cup. *(PA Images/Alamy Stock Photo)*

Jamie: Barcelona's Lionel Messi must be the best player in the modern era and among the greatest footballers of all-time. *(Photo by David Ramos/Getty Images)*

Harry: Three generations of football! Together with Harry Sr and Mark (second left).

I loved to have in through the gates at Chadwell Heath training ground. Every week, he'd be there; I'd tell the guys to let him in, he'd come and watch us put the lads through their paces, and then afterwards he'd come up to my office, have a cup of tea, and let me know in no uncertain terms what he thought about some of the players and how we'd been playing. I loved it as much as he did. That gentleman's name was Albert Chamberlain. The first manager I ever had.

Thanks, Albert.

Chapter 4

Overseas Revolution

JAMIE

Exotic. That's the word that springs to mind when I think of the few overseas players plying their trade in England when I was a kid. I say a few, but actually it's a couple. Ossie Ardiles and Ricky Villa, two World Cup-winning Argentines who came to Tottenham, intrigued the nation, winning hearts and minds, before helping to pave the now well-trodden path for overseas players into the English game.

I was too young to remember the 1978 World Cup, and too young to recall the immediate impact that these two new players had on the game, but I can imagine the press frenzy when they crossed an ocean to play for Spurs; two guys who had just helped their country become world champions.

English teams were doing great at the time. Liverpool were Europe's elite club, Nottingham Forest were about to join them, but in their squads, back then, a cultural difference meant a Scot asking for a square sausage with his fry-up. Suddenly here were two South Americans, with patchy English, but clearly very eloquent with the ball at their feet.

My first memories of them are in 1981, and the FA Cup final. The Chas & Dave song 'Ossie's Dream (Spurs Are on Their Way to Wembley)', and something about his knees going trembly. Ardiles had been the standout player. He had settled in quickly, and I remember watching him and Glenn Hoddle in a Spurs midfield that looked so cool, so different. Glenn with his shirt untucked from his shorts, Ossie with his socks rolled around his ankles, but both able to manipulate the ball so sweetly over the muddy pitches of England.

That FA Cup final was so memorable, and as good as Ardiles was in helping Spurs get there, it was Ricky Villa who stole the headlines and made the memories. I had been to Wembley the previous year for the final, with my brother and my dad, to see West Ham beat Arsenal, but to mainly see our uncle, Frank. That felt familiar. There's Uncle Frank! Yes, he's lifting the FA Cup and yes he's showing us his winner's medal after the game, but it's still Uncle Frank. It was as close to home as it could get.

In 1981, it felt different. There's that word again. Exotic. In the replay, the Wembley floodlights on, it's late in the game, 2–2. Ricky Villa picks up the ball some thirty yards from goal. He moves forward, he's into the box, he goes past one, lovely but now he'll pass, that's what players do, he goes past two, OK, he'll check back now, he cuts inside, past another, 'Still Ricky Villa' shouts John Motson and I'm joining him, the keeper comes rushing out, he still might square it, but no, he slots it under him. It's the winning goal. In a cup final. Unbelievable. Love it.

That was different. Months later, Ossie Ardiles was doing his rainbow kick (when a player flicks the ball up using his heel over his head – they call it the *lambreta* in Brazil) in the movie, *Escape to Victory*. Then, in 1982, I sat transfixed at foreign stars at that summer's World Cup. Suddenly the game was about so much more than British footballers, suddenly the game was in multi-cultural technicolour. It was like going from Kansas to the land of Oz, and it was only going to get brighter . . .

HARRY

I took my coaching job at Bournemouth in 1982, and while Jamie was marvelling at Ossie and Ricky Villa, and the many foreign stars at that summer's World Cup, an 'overseas player' to us at Dean Court meant scouting a kid on the Isle of Wight.

I remember Spurs getting the two Argentinians in. Having won the World Cup in Buenos Aires just weeks before, the double transfer did seem big. Tottenham had only just won promotion back to the top tier, they weren't a particularly great side, but suddenly all eyes were on them, and some of those eyes were not so approving. There were those that felt that looking abroad was denying British players their rightful place in the league; questions were even raised in Parliament about it. For the players to get permission to come to White Hart Lane a law going back decades had to be overruled by the European Economic Community. That's how big a deal it all was.

It was that most forward-thinking of bosses at Arsenal, Herbert Chapman, who first got people talking. In 1930, Chapman was interested in a young goalkeeper, Austrian international Rudi Hiden. Hiden had been selected to play for his national side, a brilliant and innovative set of players known as the *Wunderteam*. Chapman had seen him play against England, keeping a clean sheet, and with typical disregard for what anyone else might think, he agreed a fee with his club, Wiener FC, and the Austrian was on his way to Highbury.

The only problem Herbert had was other people's opinions, and those opinions would scupper the deal. 'Offensive' was what a chairman at another, lower club called it. Offensive to British players. He even went on to call it a sign of weakness in Herbert's management. Quite a thing to say to someone like Herbert Chapman.

The Arsenal manager would not have cared less about other people's concerns, but unfortunately for him and young Hiden, the Ministry of Labour got involved, agreeing that a move like Chapman's would restrict British interests. Regulations were put in place by the FA, regulations that stayed in place until that European intervention in 1978.

Those regulations meant that a professional footballer from abroad could only play for a Football League club if he had been living in the country for two or more years. One of the great players, when I was growing up, was Manchester City's keeper, Bert Trautmann, and he managed to play because part of his last two years in the country were spent in a prisoner-of-war camp.

Bert was a fantastic goalkeeper, one of the very best around, but his journey from a German paratrooper during the war, being held in a Lancashire POW camp, to moving on to become one of Manchester City's most loved footballers, is a brilliant one. If we think of overseas players coming here and having to not only settle into a new culture but win over supporters, no one had a bigger challenge than the big German.

My old man told me about City fans threatening to boycott matches; newspaper headlines were extreme, as was the language thrown at him from a disgruntled public.

It seems like Bert won over the City fans quickly with his brilliance, but later said that it was in a game in 1950 at Fulham, his first in London, that he faced his biggest test. The capital, the most blitzed city in the country, where the newspapers were printed. It was still a place where German soldiers weren't welcome.

Standing in his goal at Craven Cottage, hearing the shouts from the crowd, it must have been tough for Bert. 'Nazi!' was the constant shout from the crowd, but what I heard was that Bert was a man of incredible character and strength, both physically and mentally, and that he shut all that out. Apparently he had a blinder that day in goal, and as he walked toward the Cottage at the end of the game, the crowd rose up and applauded him off. Talk about the power of football. Bert later said that this moment was his most memorable, even more important that winning the FA Cup and the Footballer of the Year in 1956.

Bert's story always interested me, and it was at West Ham that I had my first taste of an overseas player facing his own hurdles in the English game. I can remember the morning we all saw Clyde Best for the first time, like it was yesterday.

We had been training at Chadwell Heath. We'd finished and we're all walking past the boys' pitch. They're doing some shooing practice and having volleys at goal, and there are balls going everywhere. Then this new, big kid steps up, and bang, the ball has flown into the top corner. Us first-team lads all look at each other, and there is a collective, 'Bloody hell.'

We all stopped to carry on watching, and Clyde carried on scoring, and Ron Greenwood, as surprised as any of us, was suddenly strolling purposefully over, wanting to know who this kid is and what is his story. Once Ron came back to the first-team dressing-room we were all asking and he told us about a remarkable journey.

Living in Bermuda, the sixteen-year-old Clyde had a coach who wrote to West Ham asking for a trial. West Ham got plenty of these requests, but they replied saying, if he can get over, they'd happily have a look at him.

The night before we see him, Clyde turns up at Heathrow Airport. He makes his way to West Ham Underground station, and then starts asking passersby where the West Ham players live. He's under the impression that all of us lived together in digs or a hotel. You have to remember that in the East End in the late 1960s, Clyde's would have been one of very few Black faces, and so there he is, this big teenager, asking a very odd question.

One guy he approaches, he must be a Hammer, because he says he does know where Johnny and Clive Charles – two young lads we had who were mixed heritage – live and so he takes him to their mum's place, she takes him in, gives him a bed for the night and, with Johnny and Clive, in he comes for training the next morning.

Ron was so excited to see him, meet him, get his story, and the next weekend Clyde was in the youth team. He scored twice in that first youth-team game, and I think the opposition were asking to see his birth certificate. He was literally head and shoulders above everyone else, and with those goals, about eight weeks later he was with us, flying back across the Atlantic for a first-team tour to America. He never looked back.

It was strange for us. There were so few Black players, Clyde really was a trailblazer, and it was hard to hear some of the stick he got away from home. We were his pals, though, we loved him, a real gentle giant, a gentleman, and we all took heart from his success story.

That's what it was always nice to see, the guys that came from overseas, it was lovely to see them settle in, get their game together, show what they could do, but also to enjoy life over here, to have their family settle. It certainly isn't always easy.

With the Tottenham lads from Argentina, I think Ossie settled better than Ricky Villa, but Ricky's goal will live long in the memory. After they came, a few more followed. I remember Charlton signing Allan Simonsen in 1982, an incredible coup, because the Danish playmaker had won European Footballer of the Year in 1977. Bobby Robson at Ipswich did great business back in 1979 too when he got Arnold Mühren and Frans Thijssen over from the

Netherlands. What a great pair they were and they helped Ipswich win honours. Great footballers.

As a young player, my first, even slight connection to overseas football was through an Englishman. Luther Blissett came to Bournemouth in 1988, when I was just fifteen, but was still in the squad when I started to play. Growing up, I loved Italian football. I loved everything about it. The players and their star quality, I loved the stadiums, I wanted the kits, and by the time Luther was with us, AC Milan, the club he had played for out there, were, under Arrigo Sacchi, becoming one of the greatest club sides anyone has ever seen.

Juventus were my team. I loved the black and white kit. Kappa. Not the usual Umbro or Adidas we had at home. The players were all so cool. The long, dark hair. Platini, Cabrini, Tardelli, Zoff. It all seemed so glamorous. We would go to the local Italian as a family, and Lorenzo, the owner, was a massive Juve fan, and loved that I was too.

I was a sponge for information about the game out there, and while I could ask Lorenzo about the club I liked, it was Luther who filled me in about the training methods, the players, the ways in which it was different. Luther was great and would talk to me about the subtle and not so subtle differences between the two countries.

There was a pair of boots that players wore out there. Ray Wilkins had them, having played for Milan as well.

As an apprentice, I would clean Luther's boots; his were Puma Kings, lovely, but I desperately wanted the Italian ones. Pantofola d'Oro they were called. Black. Beautiful kangaroo leather. Classy. As perfect for an impressionable teenage footballer to look at as the Italian game itself.

I would ask Luther about the lifestyle, and I remember how I was fascinated in Luther's stories about pasta. He was always going on about pasta, and how good it was for us. Some people might have been interested in the possibility of Ferraris and Versace suits. I wanted to know about soft leather football boots and a nice bowl of Amatriciana.

A lot of British players, like Luther, made the move to Italy, Spain and Germany. I think they all, in one way or another, found small differences. Luther used to joke about not being able to find Rice Krispies, and I remember Graeme Souness telling me about arriving to play in Genoa for Sampdoria. They had been training hard in his first summer. Long, hot, northern Italian days, and after one session, going back on the coach, Graeme grabbed an ice-cold bottle of Peroni for the journey. Just the one. A reward for his hard work, just like he would have back home.

He got on the bus, holding the bottle, cracked it open, put it to his lips, and noticed that his new teammates were looking at him like he was holding a gun. He took a gulp, but then his manager Eugenio Bersellini, a coach known for new fitness methods, approached him and said should he see him with a drink around the team again, he would simply not play.

Coming from Liverpool, and the social side to his team there, that must have been a shock, but Graeme got on with things, and like anyone moving to another country, it's all about adapting. That's not always easy. My old mate Jim Smith had an Argentinian World Cup-winning colleague of Ardiles and Villa's at Birmingham City. His name was Alberto Tarantini, a defender who was only at St Andrew's for a season. Jim would say that the player was very reliant on him, not only as his football manager but as someone who could arrange cars, houses and other administrative matters. They grew quite close because of it, but I often felt for these guys, especially when I was at West Ham, because we often threw them into the deep end.

One example was the Chilean centre-half, Javier Margas, who we got after the 1998 World Cup. He arrived with his wife, we gave him the car, sorted the house, but that was really it back then. Here's where we train, here's where you live, these are the times you need to be in, and that's about it. Players and their families were really expected to settle themselves in, whereas now there is far more support, and player liaisons in place to help them all settle.

Javier's wife found it very hard. No friends, no family, no English, and no idea where she was. From Chile to

Essex. Not the most familiar surroundings. She took the kids and went home and that left Javier a bit lost. He moved out of the house, and into a hotel off the M25 in Waltham Abbey. We would go and check in on him, because we knew his head had gone a bit. You can't blame him, really.

Myself and Peter Storrie, the chief executive, arranged to head to the hotel to see him and try to help, and when we got there, the receptionist told us he was in his room, and so we headed to it. We knocked on the door, but no response. We went back to reception, they hadn't seen him leave, but he wasn't answering his phone and so they let us into his room.

The window was open, but no Javier. He had taken his passport, but all his clothes and his kit were left. He had opened the window, leaped from the first floor to the grassy grounds below, and he had done a runner from the hotel and back to Chile. Peter went after him, but he wasn't coming back to us, and in the end we sold him to his old club, for considerably less than the £1 million we paid.

When I started at Liverpool, the amount of foreign players in the game was still very low. When the Premier League began in 1992, there were only thirteen in the whole league, and while the likes of Eric Cantona and Andrei Kanchelskis would play major roles in Manchester

United's early Premier League success, my club wasn't in a major hurry to look abroad for its players.

We'd had Jan Mølby since 1984, but the big Dane just seemed like a streetwise Scouser, we had Glenn Hysén, the classy Swedish centre-half, who was just finishing when I first got into the team, and the only other overseas player was Ronny Rosenthal, from Israel. I loved Ronny. We used to call him 'The Rocket'. Strong, powerful, he used to get his head down and just go at defenders. His shoulders were so broad, he looked like he had left the coat hanger in his shirt.

I was actually playing when he became infamous in September 1992 with an open goal missed at Villa Park. As he went through and rounded the keeper, I actually turned away to celebrate, fantastic, it's a goal, but then I heard the roar of the home crowd, and realised it hadn't gone in. Ronny would have taken a bit of stick for that, but he was great in the dressing room and soon could laugh it off.

Liverpool were perhaps the slowest of the 'big' clubs to look abroad. While Cantona, Jürgen Klinsmann, Ruud Gullit, Dennis Bergkamp and Gianfranco Zola arrived in our game, we didn't rush into it. Souness knew the European game very well, but his big signings were about capturing British talent. Dean Saunders, Mark Wright, Paul Stewart and Nigel Clough were all great players, but while the team struggled and Souness left his post in 1994, there was a new set of younger players coming through.

Take Nigel Clough. A great player, signed to replace Peter Beardsley, his role to find those pockets of space and play off Ian Rush. What Graeme didn't know when he signed him, though, was that in the youth team there was a rascal called Robbie Fowler. Steve McManaman had broken through, Barnes and Rush were there, I was playing, and so the nucleus of Roy Evans's side was very much from these isles.

Cantona, Zola, Bergkamp were all fantastic forwards, able to find and create space. Cantona changed so much for United and for our game, a real force of nature, and you could sense that the country's footballing public were embracing new cultures, new ways of doing things. Cantona with his collar up, smouldering eyes, all Gallic attitude. Bergkamp, steely Dutch vibes, ice in his veins. Zola, all Italian skill and flair.

The thing is, we had Steve 'Macca' McManaman doing similar things. Like those three, he was about exploiting space, about beating defenders; it's just that he did it with a Scouse accent rather than a European one and so perhaps it was not celebrated quite as much.

Liverpool's first big overseas signing was the Czech player Patrik Berger. A star of the 1996 European Championship, Paddy was a fantastic player. What a left foot he had. An absolute wand. Robbie's was something else, and in training we'd all just stop and clap sometimes, but Paddy's left peg was right up there.

I sometimes roomed with Paddy, and he was a great lad. Quiet, unassuming, but he never got into the nights out that we might have. He was that good looking, I hoped he would join us. What a wingman he would have been, but he preferred a quiet night in. He did take pleasure from me teaching him English swear words, and in turn my knowledge of Czech profanities grew too.

There was a lot to learn from the guys coming to play here, more than just various unsavoury words. I remember talking to my cousin, Frank, when he moved to Chelsea, and asking what it was like to work with Zola. It did seem to me that most of the big overseas names were moving to London, and there might have been a tinge of jealousy about that.

You'd get the odd one like Fabrizo Ravanelli up in Middlesbrough, and the image of Faustino Asprilla arriving at Newcastle – his long fur coat keeping him warm from the incessant north-east snow – always made me laugh, but it was mainly the capital that attracted the bigger names.

Frank would tell me all about Gianfranco – yes, about the skill on show every day in training, but also just how professional he was. Frank might join a few of the English lads for an afternoon out after training, nothing messy, but a few beers in a local, and then they would be just that little bit sluggish the next day. With Gianfranco

Zola around, doing all sorts around them, Frank quickly wanted to be at his level for every single session.

Frank wanted to compete, so slowly and surely those post-training pints disappeared, the levels went up, and the whole team benefited. I think that's what happened at most clubs. Some might have thought that the British players would try to get the foreign lads involved in their drinking clubs, but actually it was us being influenced by them.

A Wednesday at the Paradox club, or a Saturday at the Conti, began to be replaced with a meal and a glass of wine. When Macca went to Real Madrid in 1999, it was all about a small beer with a nice plate of *jamón* or stuffed peppers. It all just seemed much more civilised. Times were changing.

We were all learning, not just about professionalism, nutrition and all of that, but about the world and other cultures. We didn't go to university or college, but through football we learned so much about people's religions, their prayers, when and why they fasted. At Liverpool, we had Titi Camara and Rigobert Song, two fantastic lads, who would come in, blast out this brilliant African music, all very high tempo, they would be dancing about the place, and you couldn't help but be swept up with them. I loved it.

I had Titi and Rigobert at West Ham in 2000, and they were smashing lads. Always upbeat, always in with a smile, but I have to say, that as a manager, that was not always the case. As bright as those guys could be, I often had to deal with overseas lads who'd rather be anywhere else.

I have mentioned Javier Margas and that I could actually sympathise with his issues and his loneliness, but I had less pity for a particular player, whose name has always been put to me by those wanting to know about my less successful purchases from abroad.

Marco Boogers. A name to send shivers up the spine of most Hammers fans. Mine too. With the new season starting soon, in the summer of 1995, we were desperate for a new striker. We had looked at a few English guys in the lower leagues but the prices we were being asked to pay were silly. I was then shown a video-reel of Boogers. He was at Sparta Rotterdam, and in these clips he looked good, a goalscorer.

It was against my instincts to only go on video footage, as I would rather meet a player, find out about him, but it was all about timing, about the money the Dutch club wanted being half of what English clubs were asking for, and so we swallowed it, and made the move happen.

It wasn't long before we knew we had made an error. The players didn't take to him from the off, he didn't train well, and when he was sent off in his second game for kicking Gary Neville (the only kick he had in the game, by the way), he began to complain about being depressed, soon went home to Holland to clear his head and we never saw him again. It was a mistake on my part, one caused by slight panic, but even some of the guys who we knew a lot more about, and who we thought would be perfect, didn't work out.

Florin Răducioiu was one of those. What a striker Florin looked. A star of the Romanian team at the 1994 World Cup, and a regular goalscorer at international level. When I heard we could get him from Espanyol in 1996, we jumped at the chance. Quick, good in the air, experienced and successful in both Serie A and La Liga.

He comes to us, he scores against Manchester United at Upton Park, but I already had my doubts. What surprised me was how unprepared he was for the physicality of the English game. We played a pre-season match at Torquay and their centre-half was dishing it out a bit, and Florin came in to the dressing room, moaning.

It surprised me. The Torquay guy, an old pro called Jon Gittens, hadn't even been that rough, and Florin had, after all, played in Italy and Spain, leagues in which defenders back then took pleasure from tackles from behind that weren't necessarily designed to win the ball. I was standing in that dressing room, listening to him, thinking, this isn't going to work out. What's he going to be like when Tony Adams introduces himself to him in a proper game? It wasn't long before Florin was heading back to Spain.

I have to point out that I had many great guys from overseas over the years but, in those early days, it could be a bit of a culture shock between management and player. One of the biggest characters we had was Paulo Futre from Portugal. What a coup that was. Paulo was a terrific player. One of the real modern talents. Ron Atkinson, who managed him at Atlético Madrid, said that he would be in his all-time XI, which shows you the sort of talent we had on our hands when we brought him over from Milan in 1996.

Unlike Răducioiu, Paulo was very keen to take on English defenders, but what we didn't realise was that his work depended on a few stipulations. One was the number on the back of his shirt. With the start of the new Premier League, squad numbers had become a thing, and on the first game of the season, on a boiling hot day at Highbury, they caused us a headache.

The team was named, and Eddie Gillam, our kit man, handed out the shirts. Paulo received his and it went straight back to Eddie . . . with force. I turned to Paulo and asked what the problem was. 'Eusébio ten, Pelé ten, Maradona ten.' A pause. 'Paulo Futre ten. Not fucking sixteen.'

Uh-oh, we have an issue. I smiled and simply explained, in a calm manner, that we now had squad numbers, the number ten was taken by John Moncur, and that he has to wear sixteen.

'I no fucking wear number sixteen. Futre is ten. Futre ten at Benfica, Futre ten at Atlético Madrid, Futre ten at AC Milan, Futre ten at West fucking Ham.'

It's less than forty-five minutes until kick-off on the first game of the season, the teamsheets have been handed in to the officials, and I am having this conversation.

'Paulo, there is nothing we can do now. We are kicking off shortly, let's focus on today, and on Monday we will see what we can do with the league about making the changes. We'll need their permission.'

None of it is working. 'Futre ten,' he says again, and this time I am losing my patience. I hand him the shirt. 'Paulo, get dressed, we have a massive game, I don't need this.'

'Fuck number sixteen!' he shouts. The shirt is thrown to the floor, and his boots are kicked against the wall. That's it.

'All right, fuck off then,' I say. 'Go on, get out of my sight.'

And he did. He got his gear and he walked out of Highbury.

It meant I had to go to the referee and say that my assistant, Frank, had filled in the teamsheet wrong, and that Paulo wasn't even in England but having treatment on an injury in Portugal. Fortunately he bought my white lie and we got on with the game. It wasn't the end of the matter, though.

Paulo came in on the Monday, this time with lawyers, and we thrashed out a way of making him happy. Basically, John Moncur, a great lad, agreed to swapping and we were able to sort it with the Premier League. Paulo was grateful enough to offer John the use of his beautiful villa (the house number was of course, number ten) in the Algarve overlooking the most beautiful golf course. I'm not sure he got to use it though because, just months later, Paulo was off back to Madrid, having played a handful of games for us. Great player, wrong time. That can often happen.

It was after Gérard Houllier got the Liverpool job on his own in November 1998 – having shared the job with Roy Evans for just a few months before Roy resigned – that the club became far busier in the overseas market. In this first full summer, he bought in Didi Hamann, Vladimír Šmicer, Titi Camara, Sami Hyypiä and Sander Westerveld. All of them were welcome additions, all of them great pros, and you felt that, by bringing them, our French manager was really starting to make his mark.

Gérard was great for the young English players at the club too, bringing in that continental approach, and being a former schoolteacher, he was able to communicate with the lads, even if that meant a firm pep talk. He was great with Michael Owen and Jamie Carragher and then, when he had Steven Gerrard, a new young superstar in the ranks, the good advice continued.

Gérard had noticed that there might still be a temptation to continue to have the odd beer now and then. The Frenchman pulled Stevie aside and said, 'You can't put diesel in a Ferrari.' We all liked that one, and took heed of his wise words.

The old-school train of thought was that any problem within the squad should be dealt with in-house, and that was usually over five pints in the local. Gérard brought in a new way of doing things, and hired a great coach who had also been in the French national team's set-up. Patrice Bergues was a very clever man, a good man, I liked him a lot, and he was able to take the temperature of the squad, be a shoulder to cry on, a policeman and an agony uncle.

Gérard, that schoolteacher still in him, was all over us when it came to doing the right thing. If we even farted in training he was on us, and because of his eye for detail the standards improved and the squad won trophies.

The game was changing in as much as overseas players were now fixtures in the English game. What didn't change was the age-old battle in the midfield and since I had started in there, playing with the likes of John Barnes, the feeling was always that we had to get the better of that area, and in doing so we would have a great chance of winning football matches.

It could be Tim Sherwood and David Batty at Blackburn, later Batty and Rob Lee at Newcastle; Paul Ince and Roy Keane at Manchester United became Paul Scholes and Keane, while at Liverpool, from 1997, it became Incey in there with me.

But then came the overseas players and, while they might have arrived with reputations for sheer flair, we soon got to know that the likes of Gus Poyet at Chelsea and then Spurs and Olivier Dacourt at Everton and Leeds came with a firm attitude that very much meant business.

That was fine, but the one I dreaded playing, especially away from Anfield, was Manchester City's Georgi Kinklazde. If he was on his game at Maine Road and the crowd got right behind him, he would be in the mood to try his tricks, and if you got it wrong when trying to stop him, he had the ability to make a fool of you.

The two big game changers in the midfield were Manu Petit and Patrick Vieira at Arsenal. Two mountainous men, loads of ability and experts in the dark arts. Roy Keane was a fantastic footballer, he had everything, but I preferred pitting my wits against him than I did Vieira. Not because I felt that the Frenchman was a better footballer, there was nothing between them, but Patrick could be a bit spiteful, Manu too, and things could be left on you if their mood turned.

Patrick was especially volatile. I knew not to let him lose his rag. Sometimes you want to wind your opponent up. You see they are on the edge and so you try to press the right buttons. I remember playing Arsenal when I was at Southampton with Dad in 2005. Robin van Persie was a young and gifted striker but, in a tetchy game, I said to Dad and the lads at half-time, we can get at this kid. We'd had David Prutton sent off, and Graeme Le Saux had had some fisticuffs with van Persie, but in the second half we were cute about it, winding him up, and lo and behold, he lost his temper and saw red.

I wouldn't try all that with Vieira. Don't make him angry. If you do, he will go up a few gears. He seemed to thrive off the battle, and the more confrontational those battles were, the better he seemed to play. Instead, I'd be in his ear, telling him how well he was playing, what a good player he was, pouring on the charm. Patting him on the back, just keeping him at a level, and we might have a chance.

One of the coolest overseas players we had at Liverpool was Sami Hyypiä. The big Finnish centre-half was one of the strongest players I've seen, and I would argue one of the greatest overseas players Liverpool have had. I loved him, but it was actually a show of emotion from him that made me realise that the game had very much changed.

We were winning at Southampton, we'd been good but, being only one goal up, the lead was a precarious one. Sami went to play a ball inside, when perhaps he should have safely played it down the line; we lost the ball and Southampton equalised. It was gutting because we should have won.

We come in and, understandably, all of us including Sami are down. Then Phil Thompson walks in. Gérard's assistant, old-school and very furious. Thommo hammers Hyypiä. Old centre-half to new. I grew up in the game in the lower leagues and I have seen far worse rants from coaches, but still it was a fairly lively one, not a full paint-stripper, but loud and aggressive enough for Gérard to eventually say, 'OK, Phil, you've made your point. Enough now.'

But then Sami spoke back. I could see Thommo's words and hostility had got to him, so much so that there were tears forming in his eyes. 'You can't talk to me like that,' Sami said, his voice cracking with emotion. 'You can't talk to me like that, not ever. Only my father can talk to me like that.'

I was sat there, and I was thinking, 'Wow! Here is a guy from Finland, and he is not having a good old English verbal battering.' As I say, dressing rooms all over the country had been home to far worse. Coaches and managers have spat and screamed, for decades, but now, Sami's emotional response proved things were changing forever.

You see it today. A recent video of Vincent Kompany, when he was managing Burnley, screaming at a young pro during training drew shock and horror, and while Vincent's actions were again far from as bad as I had witnessed in my youth, the reaction underlined how rare a good managerial roar has become.

I certainly wondered at times at how Dad was coping with modernity. Not the worst shouter I have ever come across, he could bottle things up and blow his top eventually. At Bournemouth, we had a tray of sandwiches in the dressing room for after the game, and I have seen

Dad take some post-match frustrations he may have had out on it, and many of us have worn some ham, cheese and pickle before running off to the showers.

I only remember kicking one plate of sandwiches and that was at West Ham. I was having a post-match rant and Don Hutchison was going on and on. I told him to be quiet, but on and on he went, having his say. Eventually I lost it and kicked this plate, and Don had a cheese roll on his head. The funny thing was, he was still talking.

As a manager, you learned to deal with some of the overseas players slightly differently. I had heard stories from Manchester United about how Sir Alex Ferguson would give Eric Cantona far less grief than some of the British lads. If they were going out for an occasion that required a black tie, Eric might turn up in a lemon-coloured suit with white trainers. Sir Alex would smile and say, 'You look nice, Eric.'

Eric was the game changer for Ferguson. He just nudged everything forward at Old Trafford, and I get that Sir Alex wanted to handle this thoroughbred with, not necessarily a softer touch, but one that just suited the Frenchman's unique character.

I had a similar guy at West Ham. As I said to Sir Alex on the phone that time, Paolo Di Canio was among the most gifted footballers I ever managed. I quickly discovered that no day was the same with him around, and so there was no point trying to manage his personality. Sometimes he was the happiest man in the squad, the next he was the grumpiest. Anything could make him flip.

We once got a new away kit. It was navy blue. Paolo didn't like it. He hated it and it gave him the right hump. 'We look like Wimbledon,' he shouted at me.

'Sorry, Paolo,' I said. 'Nothing we can do about it unless you want to reimburse all the fans who have bought it.' It took a while for him to get over that one.

Sometimes, his mood could improve far quicker. The infamous match at Upton Park in February 2000 when Bradford were beating us 4–2 was one such occasion. The scoreline was frustrating enough, but that afternoon, Paolo was denied three blatant penalty decisions. He was furious, coming to the dugout and saying, 'The referee no like me.'

He might have had a point because they were among the worst decisions I've ever seen. It was the last one, though, that sent Paolo spiralling. He caught my eye and gestured to come off. No way. We needed a goal. 'Get on with it,' I told him.

Instead, he sat down near us, crossed his legs and his arms, and said, 'I don't play no more.'

That was different. My star player sat in front of me, like a kid on a playground, refusing to play. 'Paolo, get up, this is embarrassing, you're making a show of yourself, get up.' Years of experience had taught me that the fans would turn on him, the crowd would get toxic and the game would be definitely lost. Instead, due to Di Canio's special character, the fans loved him, whatever, and instead of booing, they began to sing his name.

Suddenly, like some superhero, Paolo is up and sprinting around like a mad man. We finally win a penalty, he grabs the ball from Frank Lampard who usually takes them and makes it 4–3; he then dribbles through their team and sets up Joe Cole, who makes it 4–4, and then Frank scores a late winner. An incredible day and an insight into what we had on our hands at West Ham.

Paolo was full of surprises. One was his taste in music. We were going to an awards dinner. Paolo had, not surprisingly, won something and so off we went. We were told that the Kemp brothers, Martin and Gary, were handing out the award, and you should have seen Paolo's face light up. 'Oh my God, oh my God,' he kept saying. I'd never seen him so excited.

It turns out that Paolo Di Canio loves Spandau Ballet, and when he met the lads, he was the most animated I ever saw him. 'Oh my God, I went to see you in Rome,' he enthused. 'I went with a ticket one night, and then the next, I had no ticket so I sneaked in, got caught by police, and beaten up.' The Kemps couldn't believe it.

Welcome to my world. It was never dull.

Much was made of the gamesmanship that these overseas players might bring with them. Jürgen Klinsmann arrived

at Spurs in 1994 with a reputation for throwing himself about, but his debut goal and that celebration when he flung himself to the floor immediately won some hearts and minds.

It was also Paolo Di Canio, in 2000 while with Dad at West Ham, who disproved the theory that overseas players would try to win by any means necessary. Everton away, the ball comes over, it's a great chance to win the game, but Paolo catches the ball to stop play because the Everton keeper is injured. Wow! Dad had to go to the cameras after the game to say what a great bit of sportsmanship that was, and how refreshing it was. I knew though that he, like the West Ham players, would have been spitting, but that's Paolo, brilliant and unpredictable.

I was fuming at that one. Paolo came into the dressing room after the game, and his teammates were all in his face, asking why? They were furious and, in the heat of the moment, so was I. Of course, Paolo couldn't have cared less. He won the FIFA Fair Play award that night. I would have rather won the three points at Goodison Park.

If Paolo's incredible talent came with a volatile personality, the other true overseas great I had, Luka Modrić at Spurs, couldn't have been more different. Luka was the easiest player to manage, just a supreme talent, and the nicest of men. Don't get me wrong, I adore Paolo, and love catching up with him, but he just was far more fiery than the little Croatian.

Luka could unlock a game, and he never gave the ball away. There were far more physical midfielders around. I may have initially been concerned when we faced the likes of Michael Essien at Chelsea, and the likes of Arsène Wenger had his doubts about how he might cope in our game, but through sheer skill he took it all in his stride when he arrived in 2008. What a passer of the ball, what a great footballing mind. He's right up with the best overseas players to have played in the Premier League. It was no wonder that I took so many calls from clubs wanting to sign him, and it's no wonder I kept saying no.

I would bet that Luka Modrić will have enjoyed playing for Dad as much as Dad enjoyed managing him. I've always said, if you can play, then Dad is a dream manager and Luka sure could play. The question is, though, who is the best overseas player to grace our game? It's so hard. Today, there are stars illuminating our game. Mo Salah at Liverpool has produced incredible goalscoring numbers from the right of his side's attack, and will go down as a true Anfield great.

Kevin De Bruyne is the best midfielder I have ever seen in the Premier League era. Not overseas midfielder, just the best player in his position, and he continues to be

a joy to watch. Another one who can just strike the ball so cleanly. I love to watch him.

If you ask me who is the best, though, I can't see past Arsenal's Thierry Henry. Cristiano Ronaldo is right up there and he might be slightly overlooked because of what he went on to achieve at Real Madrid. He did win the Ballon d'Or while at Manchester United, though, and the way he went from that skilful teenager, full of tricks, to this mad physical specimen, still so skilful but now also all power, was incredible.

I remember that free-kick he scored against Dad's Portsmouth team at Old Trafford in 2008. He's smashed it, but hit it in such a way that it looped over the wall and left David James with no chance. The next morning at training grounds all over the country, players would all have been trying it out, and some balls would have got lost that day, I can tell you.

Henry though . . . it has to be Thierry Henry. He was such a game changer and made that Arsenal team something different. The way he glided to the left, how seamlessly he did it. It's all the rage for wingers like Mo Salah to play wide and cut in on their favoured foot, but Thierry was the first to take our breath away.

I have sat with Thierry and asked him about how Arsène Wenger came up with the idea, what tactical genius went on, but he told me that it was never even spoken about, that it just happened, and that Arsenal team of the early 2000s were just allowed to be themselves.

That side, because of Thierry's ability to glide left, became unstoppable at times. Ashley Cole could overlap on the outside or inside, and Robert Pires could make his runs from the left to central positions, and back fours often had too many questions to answer.

My mate Jamie Carragher certainly had his work cut out when he played at right-back for Liverpool, and Carra has called Thierry his toughest opponent. Carra wasn't slow. He had a good turn of pace but what Henry could do is move through gears, and unlike mere mortals he had three or four of them. He would sprint with you, then slow you down to almost a standstill, and then go again. That is almost impossible to defend against.

What is certain is that the influx of overseas footballers has been the making of England's domestic game. From players to managers to fans, we can all agree that they have charmed us, they have made us smile and they have made us drool at the sheer levels of skill they bring to English football. So much so that, today, overseas footballers are every bit as much of our game as a busy Christmas, or the smell of frying onions.

Plus ça change, as they say over the Channel.

Chapter 5

My Boy

HARRY

'It's in the genes . . .' That's what I have always heard. As Jamie's talent blossomed and he went from playing with me at Bournemouth to Liverpool and winning England caps, the usual response, by those familiar with my own playing days, is that it simply had to be genetic. Perhaps they have a point. After, all, my own brother-in-law, Frank Lampard Snr, who married my wife's sister, Pat, hears the same comment when people compare his career to his son, Frank Jnr. 'It's all in the genes . . .'

Is it though? When you think about it, there are thousands of professional footballers, and not many of their sons follow their footsteps into the pro game. The percentage in fact must be very low and Frank and I, over a meal and a glass of wine, have often pondered over the fact that both of our boys became international footballers. Over time, we have come up with a theory, that genetics must surely come into it, but unfortunately neither of us can take any of the credit. It's all down to Sandra and Pat's lot.

Whatever it was, I could tell very early that Jamie was going to be a footballer. We were living in the States in the late 1970s, I was playing for the Seattle Sounders, and he, like his brother Mark, constantly wanted a ball at his feet. Mark was a great player and I'm sure would have had a pro career too but for a terrible injury playing for Bournemouth's reserves, but it was Jamie whose obsession for the game truly stood out from a very young age.

The ball would be in his arms, at his feet, in his bed. To be fair, the people kicking a ball about with him were pretty talented. Mike England, the great Wales and Tottenham centre-back, was with us and would constantly play with Jamie. Then there were two World Cup winners in Geoff Hurst and Bobby Moore, two fairly decent footballers who would never say no to an eager six-year-old pulling at their shirts and asking for a game in the garden.

Jamie would come into training in Seattle with me. He loved it, a very young kid, but he loved being around the players, listening to how they talked, watching how they behaved, and in Bobby Moore there could not have been a better role model. To Jamie, it just seemed normal, kicking his ball about with arguably England's greatest footballer. Bobby never stopped loving the game so, like a big kid who had just happened to lift the World Cup a decade earlier, he was more than obliging when it came to a run around in our garden.

Back in England, on the south coast, George Best came to stay with us while he was playing at Bournemouth in 1982–3. It wasn't the best of times for George, he was struggling, unhappy with life, unhappy with his issues with drink; but being in our garden and playing football with the boys (Jamie, about nine years old by now, trying to impress him with his keepy-uppy skills), that's when he was happy, that's when you could see that smile break through his big, black beard.

Jamie's love and talent for the game were further enhanced by me, a mischievous dad who thought nothing about letting my wife think I was driving him to school, but we would head to my work (now as manager at Bournemouth), where he would change from his school uniform into his football kit, play all day with us, and then, uniform back on, head home to his unsuspecting mum.

'What did you do at school today?' was often her first question.

'Fifty keepy-ups,' was an answer that got me in big trouble.

There was something about the way Jamie addressed the ball. He was very natural, played from a very young age with his head up, loved to pass and had a great ability to strike the ball from distance. He played loads. In fact, one schoolteacher actually stopped him playing so many games, as he felt it was too much.

I would watch him and play with him, and it struck me that he had a very good chance of making it as a player. Not that I was ever vocal about it, and I certainly wasn't strict about it. Not my style really.

I would go and watch his school games and his local schoolboys' games, but I would very much stand back, away from the other parents. Watching, but never vocal. I didn't want to be the presence there, I just enjoyed observing, seeing him improve, which he did all the time. I wouldn't get involved in the coaching of his teams either, that was for other people, and I certainly wouldn't get in their way either.

Jamie was playing for an under-10s side when he was aged just six. One of the opposing guys found out and he was thrown off the team for being too young. Too young! Imagine that? It shows how good he was if the opponents were worried about a kid four years younger than theirs. The team was called Mudeford Boys Club. It was funny because Jamie was bombed out for being too young, but they used to play a goalkeeper, a fourteen-year-old, in the same team. He was small for his age but even when he used to light up a fag during the game and smoke it leaning on the goalpost, no one said a word.

Jamie got better and better. It was no surprise to us, as even when he became a teenager, it was always about the football, about the next match. He'd come home from school, he'd drop his bag in, he'd pick up his ball, and he was off. I'd bought our house for £15,000. It was nice, but it was by no means posh, and within the little housing estate we were on there were plenty of other kids to join him. It wasn't like the council estates that I grew up playing on, old bombsites where things like the pavement's kerb could be a teammate, he had a half-decent grassed area out the back, and it was an area that gave the boys that chance to do what they loved most. His mates started to go to parties, have girlfriends, maybe pick up a can of lager here and there, but Jamie was only ever thinking about his football, and making sure he was ready to play and to win.

He had been training at Tottenham from the age of eleven. A lot of clubs wanted him at that time, but he liked the guys at Tottenham and so he would travel up there, spend the school holidays there, staying with my mum and dad, and you sensed that the club were impressed with his progress, so much so that they'd get him in with the first-team guys. One of them was a particular hero of his.

Kicking the ball about with Glenn Hoddle might have been quite daunting for most young teens, but Jamie could do it relaxed in the knowledge that he'd already done it with the likes of Mooro and George Best.

I guess you could say that it was Jamie's love, or obsession, for the game and for playing matches that actually influenced his decision to knock Spurs back and join me at Bournemouth in 1990. Terry Venables was manager at White Hart Lane and was very aware of Jamie's talent, and the club made it clear, when he turned sixteen, that they wanted him to sign professional forms.

Spurs were a big club, competitive, and they had Terry, a coach respected all over Europe. It wasn't long before the manager was on the phone to me.

'We think your boy is a certainty to make it, Harry,' he said.

OK, I thought, great club, great manager, seems the logical move for my boy. The thing is, Jamie had other ideas. Jamie was concerned about getting a chance at Tottenham. He was only sixteen, but he wanted to play first-team football, he wanted to learn while playing with men, and to do that, he thought his best chance was playing for me. It was a hard phone call back to Terry.

I'm sure Terry presumed I was the one in Jamie's ear, that I was telling him to stay south with me just so he could strengthen my team, but nothing could be further from the truth. In fact, I thought Jamie was making a mistake. I thought being at Spurs with their facilities, with their players around him, with Terry himself there to learn from, would be right for him.

Jamie had always come to training with me at Bournemouth. We were in the Second Division, he played with the lads there, they liked him, and he could hold his own, so he had this sense that he could play and thrive at that level, and that the First Division, as the top league was known back then, could wait. 'I want you to go to Tottenham,' I used to say to him, but that was only my advice, I certainly wouldn't or couldn't make him do what he didn't want to do.

Terry wasn't happy, and we had a bit of a fallout. 'Tel, what can I do?' I'd say. 'He's made his mind up, I've tried to talk him around, but he just wants to play league football now.'

That was that. I had to respect Jamie's decision, it was brave, but now I was his manager, and had to decide when and how to play him.

I was probably a bit slow to throw him in. He was training great, he was mixing well with the lads and, despite his young age, he was certainly physically able to be involved, but looking back, maybe, as a dad, I just held back a bit. I never pushed my kids into anything and I think that influenced how I handled Jamie as a player.

It was Paul Miller, the former Spurs centre-half playing for me at Bournemouth, who had a word.

'You have to play him,' Paul said. 'He's the best we've got in midfield, and if he wasn't your son, he would be in.'

He had a point and so he was in, maybe not every game, but certainly a lot of them, and like everything as Jamie's dad, it was easy and a pleasure. There were never any problems, he never came home saying so-and-so said this or that, he got on with everyone, and because he was so good, those players knew he was there purely on merit.

It turned out to be the very best education. It wouldn't happen today. We grew up on reserve-team football, playing with seasoned pros. West Ham reserves would play every other Saturday when the first team were away, we'd get five or six thousand people there, and you'd play Arsenal, Chelsea or Tottenham, and there would be plenty of first-team guys involved so the standard was great. That's how you learned the game.

It's all academy stuff now, played at their facilities in front of no one, away from the first team and the manager, and the youngsters, while technically great, aren't learning much about the game and its hard knocks. I hope the loan system doesn't disappear too. I loaned Frank Lampard Jnr out at West Ham, to Swansea, in 1995. Frank went down there, he grew up there, played in ankle-deep mud at the old Vetch Field stadium, and he loved it. It made him.

Jamie certainly thrived with me, and he could handle the physical side of things. Having gone back down to the old Third Division, it was very physical. Graham Barrow was a player, a great lad, playing for Chester, who taught Jamie a thing or two. Jamie would get the ball, nice touch, and play it wide before making a forward run. There was Graham, not interested in the nice football Jamie was trying to play. Instead, he's blocking his path. Have that. Wallop. It was a learning curve, but you sensed that Jamie loved it. He was doing what he wanted to do: play. It wasn't long, though, before another very big name was on to me about him.

Kenny Dalglish, one of the true greats of British football, and in 1990, the manager of the very best team in the country, Liverpool. League champions again. Kenny, manager of a team brimming with massive names, and having listened to his very trusty lieutenant, Ronnie Moran, who had seen Jamie play for us at Birmingham, he wanted to know more and asked if Jamie would join him for a week's trial.

At the end of Jamie's first day up there, I came home from work, and there were eight messages from Kenny. I was worried that maybe Jamie was hurt. He wasn't. Kenny was impressed. 'Harry, we have to sign him.'

Here we go again. I went up there and one night over a Chinese meal, he reiterates how much they want him. I have to have the same conversation with Kenny Dalglish as I've had months before with Terry Venables. Giants of the game, and I'm breaking it to them that my boy just wants to play first-team football.

'He can do that, here,' Kenny says.

This is a midfield that boasts the likes of Steve McMahon, Jan Mølby, John Barnes, Ronnie Whelan and Ray Houghton.

'Don't be silly,' I say. 'With the talent you've got?'

Perhaps Kenny knew that his team was ageing, and that a new team might be built soon, but he was adamant that Jamie was good enough to be in and around the first team, and his chance would come. 'Quicker than you can believe.'

Jamie, now with good first-team experience with me under his belt, was interested. Kenny had been great with him, having him to stay at his house with his family, ringing us every day to chat, and soon it was little wonder that Jamie felt maybe now was the right time. Kenny actually resigned from the job not long after Jamie signed in January 1991, the obvious strains of the role over a few years that included the tragic Hillsborough disaster taking their toll, but in that short time, he had a great effect on Jamie and his career.

When you love football, it's a dream to have a boy who plays professionally but you know it's not easy, and seeing him prosper at Liverpool, seeing him become an international footballer, while knowing all the hard work he always put in, it made me very proud.

When they were young, I had made sure I got both Jamie and Mark a paper round. It gave them a bit of pocket money, but I wanted them to have a work ethic and to appreciate things. I think little things rubbed off on them, and Jamie's attitude as a kid and then as a professional footballer was always spot on.

I was never one to go on about my kids, maybe I was a bit old school in that way, but I can say now that I am so proud of both my sons, and watching Jamie play always brought me a lot of pleasure.

Unless I was managing a side he was playing against, of course. That was never easy. I don't think either of us enjoyed that. It was just weird. I remember one game at Anfield. I brought my West Ham team there, and Jamie went in on Frank Lampard. It was a heavy challenge, let's put it that way. Frank had a cut on his leg, and our dugout was up, enraged. I usually would have been too, but, well, it's my son.

Les Sealey was my goalkeeper coach. I loved Les, he was one of the game's great characters, and he's up, screaming at the ref to take some action. Frank gets seen to, and while he's down near us, Les is telling him to give Jamie one back. Again, usually, not a problem, but I am close to telling Les to calm down.

I never really thought about trying to sign Jamie during his career, it's hard enough managing a football club without having your own kid with you, but when he did come and play with me again in January 2005, I enjoyed having him there. I was at Southampton. I had gone there from Portsmouth, a move that got a bit of attention, and the job was all about keeping the club in the Premier League. Jamie was coming to the end, his knee was failing him, but he joined me for half a season, and he did so with all the same enthusiasm that he had always shown for the game. He certainly wasn't there for a last big payday, I can tell you that. We paid him peanuts.

We had some good players, and Jamie did very well. I'm not just saying that, as again, I'm the last person to praise my own kids too much, but he was, he was excellent. Professional and dedicated (he had a few cortisone injections in that knee, which tells you everything about him), Jamie had a great influence on the dressing room. If you asked Kevin Phillips, or other seasoned pros that we had like Rory Delap, they would tell you the same thing: Jamie was fantastic.

It wasn't enough to keep us up though. It was strange. We threw away some good leads, and things went against us. I am the first to say if one of my teams has been lucky. There have been games and there have been seasons when I have thought, 'Cor we were lucky to win that,' or 'How lucky were we to stay up there?' But on this occasion, I don't mind blaming a big chunk of misfortune for Southampton's relegation.

With the controversy of my moving there, it was a difficult time, but to be there with Jamie made it far more bearable. In April we went to Portsmouth, and the fixture was toxic, to say the least. We even had the police at our training ground in the week leading up to the game, telling us about their strategy on the day to keep the peace.

'If your team scores, don't jump and celebrate,' was one line that stood out.

'Don't worry, I'm not crazy,' was my reply.

On the coach in, the abuse from the streets was as bad as I've ever seen, and in the sanctuary of the dressing room, I didn't blame some of the players for having second thoughts about going out to warm up. Peter Crouch was with me, and also had been at Portsmouth. He knew he was going to get some stick. He had been nursing a tight hamstring all week, and he quickly declared himself unfit to play. I didn't blame him!

It was a cauldron of hate and, for my part, I felt guilty for putting my family through it all. Jamie was, as ever, staying focused, being professional, but he must have known what was waiting for him out there, and that every time he got on the ball, he would be greeted with boos. I was so impressed with him that day. He even found time to give me a pep talk before we went out.

'Come on, Dad, walk out there with your head held high,' he said. 'Whatever they shout at you, you haven't done anything wrong.' That was typical of Jamie. He's about to play the game, one that will be very tough, but he's thinking of me.

It was no surprise that we got beat heavily that day, they were a great side, but having Jamie there made it bearable.

Our most memorable win was probably the 2–0 victory against a Liverpool team who would win the Champions League a few months later. That was a nice day for Jamie especially. He showed that he was still competing well against the very best but, behind the scenes, his knee was bad. We'd play an away game, get back at two in the morning and Jamie would go straight to the physio to have two or three hours' treatment on it. The knee was hanging on by a thread and, at the end of the season, he had to pack it all in.

I look back on Jamie's professional football career with nothing but pride. It's nice that it was bookended with me as his first and last manager but, as a father, I can hold a bit of frustration on his part because he was unlucky with injuries. Injuries of course are a part of football, and Jamie would be the first to say that, but his came at tricky times, just when he was playing his best football for both Liverpool, and in the case of the European Championship in 1996, England too.

In the end, Jamie went on to fulfil his dreams. He played for a club like Liverpool, he captained them, and he played for his country. What I am most proud of, though, is the manner he did it, and the man he became.

I can still see him kicking the ball about the garden, the sun coming down and his mum having to call him in, very much against his will.

I knew then that he'd go far. Just don't give my genes the credit!

Chapter 6

1996 and All That

JAMIE

'Dad is gonna kill me!'

Those were my first thoughts as the papers were delivered under my hotel door, on a Monday morning in the summer of 1996. There I was on the front pages, in more trouble alongside teammates who were already very much in the nation's bad books.

It was two days after the opening game of the European Championship in England. We had ground out a disappointing draw with Switzerland. Terry Venables, our manager, hadn't panicked, though, not his style really, and instead he told us to go home for the night, have a day off, get away from the hotel, from the squad, get away from all the pressure.

I wasn't going to travel all the way back to Liverpool where I lived, Mum and Dad had been at the match but were going away that night, I was single at the time, and so I went up to Essex and stayed with my cousin, Frank Jnr.

We were indoors with his sisters, Clare and Natalie, and we decided to pop out to a club in Ilford called Faces. Now, looking back, that wasn't the wisest idea but it was just something to do. We weren't drinking loads, nothing major, just a couple of hours to unwind. But, after about an hour, Teddy Sheringham walks in, and then Sol Campbell.

News gets out, some photos are taken and when we arrive back at the team hotel at Burnham Beeches on the Sunday night, Terry calls us in and tells us we will be on the front pages of the next day's tabloids.

And so, the following day, there it is, a front-page splash. More negative news about the England team, more disappointment, more national outrage. The country is in uproar but the first thing I am thinking about is Dad.

'Dad's gonna kill me!'

HARRY

If I had been the manager, I might have killed someone. As Jamie's dad, though, I just asked, 'Why, son? Why did you do it?' but to be honest, I knew the boys hadn't gone out and had a mad one, and I also knew that the whole squad were under a crazy spotlight. One that hadn't really been seen before. Footballers were now very much in the public eye, not just because of what they did on a football pitch, but how they lived off it. The Premier League was new and massive, and those who played in it were of interest. Who were you dating? How much were you drinking? What money were you earning? It was all new, and that squad in 1996 had to take it on the chin.

I got all that, and I understood why the public had a low opinion of us at the time. It was only a couple of weeks after the infamous 'Dentist's Chair' incident in Hong Kong, and while none of us got drunk that night after the Switzerland game (Sol doesn't even drink!), the timing was bad.

Terry told us to go out that night, in Hong Kong. We had played a couple of pre-tournament warm-up games in Asia and so, always mindful of his players and allowing them freedom to relax, he gave us the green light to go out and let off steam. He also gave us his coach, Bryan Robson, as a chaperone. When we heard Robbo was coming, a great guy who liked a night out, we knew it was game on. All of us are thinking, 'Are you sure you want Bryan Robson to lead us into battle?'

Add to that the fact that it was Gazza's birthday, and things were always going to get messy. You have to remember, the tournament was a little way off, and

Terry was great at knowing when his players needed some downtime. The problem is, it got a bit out of hand, and people were taking photos, something that rarely happened back then.

As we took it in turns on that chair, none of us had a clue we were being photographed. The tequila might have dumbed our senses, I guess. The fallout was huge, I get that, and on top of it all, there was some damage to a television screen on our plane home. Us Liverpool lads got the blame for that. Robbie, Macca and myself. Always the Scousers! It wasn't us and one day the truth will come out. Won't it, Gazza? We did shave off Gazza's eyebrows, though, when he was finally asleep. I'll admit to that. The thing is, he bleached his hair blond and you couldn't really notice it. Still disappoints me, that.

In all seriousness, I get why everyone was so upset, I get why everyone thought we were misbehaving, but that night in Hong Kong, that is still in my top-five best nights out ever. A load of mates having the best laugh. I was actually gutted that there were no pictures of me in the chair! Football's young lads, they've always been prone to a bit of mischief: I know Dad's era was full of rascals, Dad and even Bobby Moore included. The thing is, though, they didn't get caught.

The important thing here was the manager. He looked after the players. Terry was a clever man. One of the great coaches and one of the great man-managers. It had been a tough few years for English football. Graham Taylor was a great coach and brilliant guy, but I think he had found it hard to get the country behind him. Results suffered, the press were nasty, and it all needed a change.

There were a few great young coaches about. Ray Wilkins, Glenn Hoddle, Gerry Francis, Bryan Robson, all former internationals, but it had to be Terry didn't it? He had done so much, was popular with fans and journalists, and the things he had achieved at Crystal Palace, Queens Park Rangers, Barcelona and Spurs, well it had to be him.

I'd had that slight run-in with Terry when he wanted to sign Jamie at Spurs, and ultimately Jamie's decision to stay and play in Bournemouth's first team hadn't gone down too well. Terry was never one to hold a grudge for long, though, and any mad feelings didn't last long. He must have carried on rating Jamie, giving him his first cap a year before the championship.

Looking back, that decision to turn Terry and Tottenham down was a brave one. I was only young but I knew the path I wanted my career to take, and I knew that meant playing first-team football. If that meant doing it with Bournemouth, then that was fine by me. I learned loads, and getting to Liverpool eventually proved me right, I guess.

I'd been doing OK in a good, young Liverpool team. We had Robbie Fowler, Steve McManaman, Rob Jones.

The experience came with Mark Wright at the back and John Barnes in midfield with me. I remember John pulling me to one side toward the end of the 1994–5 season and saying, 'You will be an England player soon.' For John, a hero of mine, to say that? Wow. Not that I fully believed it, but it's something when someone like John thinks so.

As a parent, I was just happy that my boy's dream of playing league football for Liverpool had come true, and when that happens, of course international football has a good chance of following. I remember hearing that Terry was picking Jamie for England for a game against Colombia in September 1995. It was a great moment for the family. I remember telling my dad, Jamie's biggest fan, and the pride on his face was special.

It was autumn 1995. I remember getting a number: 1069. That was *my* number. That's how many players had represented England. It's not that much and your mind turns to those guys before you. Bobby Moore, heroes as a boy such as Bryan Robson, John Barnes, and Gazza. This tournament was around the corner and I'm thinking, 'I might be playing in a midfield with Gazza!'

That game, my debut against Colombia, was more famous for their keeper René Higuita's scorpion kick from my scuffed cross. I actually turned away in disgust at my effort so missed the moment but I did OK in the

game. I was by no means sure of getting in to Terry's final squad, though. I'd had a bad injury in the 1995–6 season, Liverpool lost the FA Cup final against Manchester United and I thought it might be a stretch. Rob Lee had a great season with Newcastle, but he got ill during the warm-ups. I'm not sure to this day if that swung it for me, but I was in and I was going to make the most of it.

Training had been great. It all just felt good. I felt good. I'm pinging the ball about, shots are hitting the top corner, I'm comfortable on the ball, I'm strong and I'm passing well. It doesn't happen too often but everything felt right in my game. I think I caught Terry's eye. He took me to one side and said that he had his starting XI in his mind, but to stay patient, that things would change and I'd get a chance.

If I was feeling great, the squad as a whole was far from totally content. The country was not happy with us after those reports from Hong Kong, and we had to really dig in and use our own collective bond to get through the early days of that tournament. We had that incredible camaraderie, a real top set of lads, but there was by no means a jubilant expectation that Terry's team would do well. After several mishaps in friendlies, the press were unsure and negative, the pundits didn't quite know what formation and team Terry would opt for, and the public . . . well, thanks to that Dentist's Chair, most of them presumed we were a bunch of spoilt drunks.

In the team, Alan Shearer had struggled to score for England. Two years without a goal, wasn't it? Graeme Le Saux had broken a leg, that Christmas-tree formation experimented with by Terry was being pilloried, but the manager was brilliant at shutting out all the outside noise. He was working on his team's flexibility. He wanted the squad to be adaptable. We worked on playing three at the back as well as 4–4–2. Terry might have been quietly confident, but if I said that there was this big plan and us players were well-drilled and ready to rock Europe, then I'd be lying.

As a player, though, you wanted to learn from Terry. You realised during training sessions that this man knew his stuff, and to be around him was an education. He would suggest scenarios in training, but not for the sake of it. They would then occur in practice and real games. What I especially liked about him was that he was great at explaining issues of space. Where it could be found, how to utilise it. I loved all that, and tried to take it all on board. Get in space, get the ball, and look for the likes of Gazza on the half-turn. Nothing complicated but very effective.

Going into the opening game, I was aware that some of the senior players were struggling. Not with form necessarily, but with the tension, caused mainly by the issues with the public and the press after Hong Kong. The squad was full of huge characters, most of them able to captain their clubs or their country, but there was a tangible stress around the place that got worse as the tournament got closer.

Despite a first-half goal for Alan Shearer, that tension showed and we only got a 1–1 draw from that opening game. The Swiss were organised and durable, the least perfect team to play against in the circumstances, and the cloud over us went into the following week.

Training became a bit weird after that draw. There was a lack of spark. Lots had been written about us, and it seemed to add lead to some of the legs. Sessions were flat, despite Terry, Don Howe and Bryan's efforts. I'd go as far as to say that the majority of the squad were not even looking forward to the Scotland game. That's how much was hanging on it.

For myself, I was wondering if my form might get me the nod, but Terry kept the same XI. However, he changed the formation, going with a 3–5–2 formation with Gareth Southgate stepping into a three-man midfield. It wasn't an easy first half. Scotland were really at it. Players like Gary McAllister, Colin Hendry, Gordon Durie, all on their game and not much was coming off for us. Their fans were as loud as ever, and so you did wonder how the England team would find its mojo.

Myself and Sandra were up in the stands. It had been a hard first half, not much action, hardly any space in there, but I remember the whistle going and then, a moment later, Jamie getting up from the bench, finding us with his eyes and gesturing up to say he was coming on. You could see the excitement in his eyes, and it was replicated in mine and his mum's. That was a proud and exciting moment.

I remember it well. Mouthing 'I'm coming on' up to Mum and Dad. The half-time whistle blows and, in a second, Terry tapped me on the shoulder. 'Get warmed, son, you're coming on.' Thirty years later, and I still get goosebumps thinking about that.

I went on to the pitch to warm up, and I'm gliding across it. I'm pinging the ball around, stretching, little sprints, itching to get going. The trainer tells me to get in and get ready, and as I'm running toward the tunnel, I'm not aware of my feet touching the ground. I'm so excited, I'm floating.

I then got to the dressing room, we were in the away one that day, and the first person I bump into is Stuart Pearce. At that point, I'm not aware that it is Pearce who has been subbed for me, but suddenly I am in his arms. He gives me the biggest bear hug, almost breaks my rib, and he's saying, 'Come on, son, get out there and make something happen for us.'

I always appreciated Stuart for that. Some might have sulked, some might have thrown their boots down and headed for the showers without a word, but Pearcey

seeks me out, hugs me like I'm his first-born and gives me a pep talk. It said everything, not only about Stuart Pearce's team ethic, but the squad's, and despite the lack of spark so far in the tournament, you could never discard the leadership qualities within our group.

And none came any bigger than Tony Adams. Tony was *the* captain. Tony was a colossal man among men, and despite dealing with his own personal demons that summer, he was the pinnacle when it came to pushing us towards being the team we knew we could be.

After Stuart's hug, I walk into the dressing room. It's the usual organised chaos, coaches giving individual talks, masseurs working on tired limbs, and then as I sit down to get myself ready, Tony is standing up and starts to talk. 'Lads,' he says with that big Essex twang of his. 'Lads, this is our fuckin' house. This is our fuckin' home . . .' It's a rousing start but while he's talking, he has a doctor at his feet with a needle that looks like a medieval weapon, about to go into his knee. In goes the needle, in goes the cortisone, but Tony doesn't flinch.

'This is our fuckin' house, and if these lot think they are walking in here and getting a result in front of our people, they are in for a big fuckin' surprise.'

Everyone's cheering. My mouth is agape, and not because of the size of the needle. I am, like the whole room, buzzing. Get me out there. There are no tactical pointers from Terry, and if there were I doubt we would have listened to them. I just want to take on the whole world.

I fancy a game now!

It was a special moment. I have never met anyone in football like Tony. A natural leader like I have never seen. You can't fake it, it has to be authentic, and Tony was just born to lead. If you think of the stick he took as a young footballer, it was crazy. You don't get that any more, players aren't really questioned about their ability to just play. Tony was. The donkey jibes, the back pages mocking him, but he never wavered. Self-belief, pure talent and inner strength. I wish we'd have had cameras following us around that summer to show everyone just how important Tony was to the squad. Having said that, cameras following us around in Hong Kong might not have been such a good idea.

With Tony's words ringing in our ears, we went out and began to play, and my own mood was lifted because all that good form and confidence I had felt in the lead-up to the tournament was with me on that hot and vital afternoon on the pitch at Wembley. I felt at ease. My mates were around me. Macca gliding about. Darren Anderton doing the same. Gazza starting to find pockets and wanting the ball early. Gareth Southgate has dropped into the back three, Paul Ince is behind me, and I am getting on the ball and looking for players with that commodity Terry had spoken so well of. Space.

As well as space, my greatest asset that afternoon was a lack of fear. There was no burden on me, nothing to lose, everything to gain. Coming on as substitute should be easier. You should play with the shackles off and, luckily for me, I was able to get into the rhythm early, make a few tackles and then just pick out Darren, Macca and Gazza, who were finding a bit more room. We scored through Alan again. Happy days, but you have to remember that from there it nearly went south again. We gave away a penalty and had they scored they might have held on to a draw or even nicked a win, and we are almost down and out. A squad close to being public enemies. A squad who have made a right show of themselves from beginning to end.

Instead, what follows is a moment of individual genius, the likes of which I don't think I have ever seen close up before or since. Paul Gascoigne. Gazza. A genius among us. A special man, a special player who roars forward, the living embodiment of Tony Adams's speech, and scores the most sublime goal that to this day defies logic.

Playing in midfield with Gazza, you knew that what he needed most was freedom, and it was up to us players around him to realise that. That meant being aware of his movements, appreciating that he wanted to join the attackers, getting beyond them even, and filling in any gaps he might leave. He was too potent a weapon to hinder with tactical instructions. Go on Gazza, do you what you want and cause mayhem. And that's exactly what he did.

I had the best seat in the house. The ball broke in midfield, Teddy found Darren, who was a beautiful passer of a football; he lifted the ball forward for Gazza who had made one of his third-man runs. I am drifting in behind and have the perfect view of Gazza putting the burners on. He's away, such power, upper-body power, and he is desperate to get there before the Scottish centre-half, Colin Hendry.

You have to remember that Gazza had been getting a lot of stick from the press and the fans. There was the Dentist's Chair and the drinking habits, and plenty of people wondered if his time had gone. Creatively, he was our main man but many were suggesting he was past it. I don't think Terry was interested in all of that but Gazza did have a bit to prove.

So, he gets to the ball and I am ten yards behind him, and I can't believe my eyes. He flicks the ball with his left foot, up over Hendry's big frame, and then with his right foot unleashes the most controlled volley past his Rangers goalkeeping teammate, Andy Goram. I'm not being funny, but I don't think any other player, anywhere, would have tried that.

If he'd flicked it over Hendry's head with his right foot, and then volleyed it with his right, that would have been hard enough, but to use both feet, while running at such pace, I'm telling you that is so, so hard. I don't think even Lionel Messi tries that. It's not a Messi move. Messi would have got on the ball and with a trick sat the defender down, before scoring, sure, but that trick, that goal, I cannot reiterate just how difficult a skill that was, and just what a maverick, footballing mind it takes to even try it.

That's what Gazza was. A maverick. A person and a footballer like I have never known. He was a one-off. I remember that Dad would phone me after I'd been away with England and ask me questions about the training, but mainly the questions were all about Gazza. How he trained, what skills he tried out, what crazy things he had got up to?

When it came to the latter there were usually too many to mention. Us younger lads loved him. He was a senior player but he loved to have an audience in us, and the likes of me, Robbie, Macca, we'd take it in turns to look after him, playing ping-pong or tennis. There was never, ever a dull moment.

The hotel at Burnham Beeches was all ours, so there were no guests to upset, and Gazza would have everyone, the squad, the management (most of the time), the hotel staff, all of us in stitches. He'd be up at 5 a.m. and hit the gym, doing weights. Incredible energy, and so it was no surprise when he turned the whole summer's bad press into his iconic goal celebration.

On the bus to Wembley that day, he let us know that if he scored, he was going to mimic the Dentist's Chair, and that anyone close had to spray him with the bottles of energy drink near the goal. Us lads who were out that night in Hong Kong were the first there. I wasn't going to miss this photo opportunity.

And with that moment of genius, Gazza changed the course of the summer. Not only did the once-in-a-generation piece of skill secure the win, it lifted the nation from its doubtful slumber, and by his laughing at what happened in Hong Kong, the public did too and suddenly all was forgiven. As simple as that. The country had its football team, and the team suddenly had the kind of support that might just get us close to winning something.

It was an incredible moment. Me and Sandra, sat in the stands, and you could sense something shift. The team looked great, Gazza looked world class again, Jamie was pulling the strings in the midfield and that anthem about football coming home started to be sung. Quietly at first and then the whole stadium. Well, the English fans anyway. But then, what looked like a nothing moment, and disaster.

It was a nothing moment. It was the last few minutes of the game. Incey had gone off, so I dropped a little deeper. The ball went up, over Gary McAllister's head, I jumped

and landed and it happened. I had put these inner soles in my boots. I can't even remember why. When I landed, the soles seemed to slip, and the ankle turned. I heard a loud crack and that was that. I knew it was bad. No one near me, but I have damaged my ankle badly, and straight away, I'm fearing the worst.

I was stretchered off, and when I was getting an X-ray, deep below the stands, I can hear that song. 'Three Lions' is being belted out. The song had been on the radio a bit, but now, in the ground, the fans are singing it, all of them. You could sense something change in the mood. As for my ankle, the only thing coming home was me. Although, I didn't. I wanted to stay with the group.

After the game, Terry said, get fit, you are now starting, but as pleased I was to hear his words, I knew the injury was fairly serious and so when I got the news that there was a hairline fracture, it came as no surprise. I was devastated. Devastated because I felt so good that summer and think I might have made a difference.

I am not one to blow my own trumpet, but I turned that game because I played without fear and think I would have done the same for the rest of the tournament. As I say, playing with no fear is a special weapon to have for any footballer, and I think the team certainly showed that with their next performance against the Dutch.

I had the option to go home, but I didn't want to. I had the medical treatment I needed there and, anyway,

it was like being on the best stag do, and now the team were winning that buzz about the place was only getting better. I was wearing a protective boot, and I was allowed to attend and watch training, and from a professional point of view, to be able to observe Terry and Don and their staff's training methods was so informative, and I would sit at the pitchside and take it all in.

And then the Netherlands game a few days later was a culmination of all those methods coming together, the players playing without fear, and everyone brimming with confidence. A lot is made of the flexibility of the squad and it being adaptable with formations, but players make systems, not the other way round, and the players suddenly had such belief.

I reckon that that performance against a useful Dutch team – full of stars, full of talent, some of the best in Europe – was right up there with the best I have ever seen from an England team. It must have been so exciting to be sat with the rest of the squad, near the staff, near Terry, and to take it all in.

None of us had never seen England play that well, and I am not sure I have since. On the bench as it unfolded, especially the second half, us guys were just looking at each other. No words needed. Eyebrows raised, cheeks blowing. Disbelief. Everything was coming off. Players

were wanting to get on the ball, make runs, cover for each other; the closest thing to total football I have seen England play, and it's against the Dutch.

Teddy coming off the front line, Gazza with all that freedom he relishes, Darren and Macca marauding forward, Southgate and Adams stepping out, Incey patrolling and passing, Shearer a constant threat, it was magnificent to watch. The Dutch were fortunate to keep it down to 4–1, really.

After that, the nation went crazy. At the start of the tournament we would pull out of our hotel in the team bus, and there might be twenty or thirty people along a route waving (or making other hand gestures) at us. After the Netherlands game, the streets were four or five deep, St George's Crosses everywhere, and a real enthusiasm.

The Spanish were, albeit slightly fortunately, beaten on penalties in a quarter-final game made famous by Stuart Pearce's guts, penalty success and celebration that was pure aggression, redemption and relief. Having missed his penalty six years earlier at Italia '90, to step up and take that one, with so much to lose, well on the sidelines we were probably more nervous for him than he was for himself.

Stuart's energy matched the squad's. We were in the semi-finals, we were playing Germany, and we knew that this was a massive chance to emulate the lads of 1966.

There was a real togetherness. Granted, some of the lads wanted to be playing more than they were. Les Ferdinand, for instance, he wasn't used, and you sensed he wasn't happy. That's fine. Les was one of the best strikers in the country, brilliant at Newcastle that season, but Alan is Terry's main man, he's rediscovered his goalscoring touch at international level and that's that. It's hard, you felt for Les, but what can you do? He wasn't sulking or anything like that, and we all went on to Wembley that Wednesday, 26 June, confident that we were better than Germany and could win.

We dared to think that this German team were there for the taking. No Oliver Bierhoff, Jürgen Klinsmann suspended, and our lot brimming with self-belief and roared on by a crowd willing to believe that this was it. This was '66 all over again. But, and it's still hard to take, you have to say it was a missed opportunity. They weren't the best German side of all time, far from it, and the Czech Republic in the final at Wembley would have been a very winnable game. They were decent, with players like Patrik Berger, who I would get to know well, but you'd fancy England to have beaten them.

I remember the bus journey from Burnham Beeches to Wembley. Terry had arranged for a load of our goals to be put on the coach's TV screens with Baddiel and Skinner's song on, and it got the lads going, Gazza was doing his thing and the bus was a good place to be. Not overly confident but focused, relaxed with a real sense that something great might happen here.

In the semi, we scored early with an old-school, near-post corner routine, but we let the Germans back in and from there it really could have gone either way. End to end, and then that extra-time with the Golden Goal rule, and Gazza is centimetres away from winning it for us. They had some chances too, and then it goes to penalties and we all know what happens there.

England took some great penalties to be fair, top corners, but so did the Germans. When Gareth Southgate stepped forward, there was not one sense of, 'What is he doing, taking one?' Gareth was a good footballer, could hit a ball well and, most importantly, he really wanted to take one. He had insisted, so from the bench when we saw him walking towards the spot, it was just a case of, 'OK, come on, Gareth mate.' He hit it cleanly enough, but the keeper guessed right and that's that. Just one of those things.

You immediately felt for him, because you got the situation and you realised the magnitude of what had happened and how the country would feel. Tony was great with him, leading him towards the fans in the ground and making him take the applause.

We all went back to the hotel after, and had the option of going back to our homes, but no one did. We wanted to stay one more night together, and we sat in

the hotel bar, a few beers, and we quietly talked about what had gone on, how close we had got, and to this day there is still a bond between the guys who were there that summer.

For those of us who were about in 1966, there were a lot of similarities. The way the country got behind the team, but also the tactical changes the coach made for the tournament.

I think of the 'Wingless Wonders' in '66 and how the team developed into something tactically different but successful. Terry chose to play a lot of the tournament with three at the back, and that was not really the norm, but it worked for him, and the team were able to play exactly the way he intended. I personally loved that formation. We used it at Liverpool, and were very comfortable in it. I think it's a system that promotes freedom going forward. At Liverpool, we had Macca who was able to simply roam about causing problems. In England, we had Gazza who could do exactly the same.

Terry was a visionary and it was typical of the FA not to work it out so that he could have stayed on for a while longer and take England to a World Cup. Don't forget that Terry had had the foresight to get promising young players involved that summer. He took Rio Ferdinand

and Frank Jnr from my West Ham side along to train with the senior squad, all with an eye on the future. That was very clever and not something other managers might have thought to do. It showed that he needed to be there longer, but it wasn't to be.

Don't get me wrong, Glenn Hoddle was a good young coach, but looking in as a fan, and seeing what Terry had achieved and the bond he had with that set of players, I think the powers that be should have sorted out their differences and made sure he stayed on.

We were all sorry to see Terry go, because we all loved him, and when it came to his successor, we presumed it would be Bryan Robson. It was very astute of Terry to have brought Bryan in as an assistant. Our generation of players were in awe of him as a footballer, he was doing well as manager at Middlesbrough, and it was felt that he would just slot in. The FA went with Glenn, who was a fantastic young coach, but I just think he could have got the job later, and Bryan should have been given the chance to carry on Terry's work in 1996.

But for now, it was all over, and we went back to our families and our clubs, and it's on to the next season. That's football. I was very proud to have been part of the squad, though, to have made some sort of impact in a game and on the team's fortunes.

It was a great summer. An iconic one. Britpop music, political changes coming, the St George's flag everywhere, smiling people, that song. It didn't come home, it still hasn't, but my word, we had a good go at it . . .

Chapter 7

The Greatest Match

HARRY

If we're going to talk about the great matches, let's start with what is still the greatest match the Premier League has seen. Liverpool v. Newcastle in April 1996. I was there, I came up to watch Jamie play that night. What a football match. End to end, loads riding on it, great players, great goals, a dramatic finish.

JAMIE

It was some night, but it was only afterwards when we watched the game back that us players realised just how entertaining a match it was. When you're playing, you sense that chaos is happening, but you are so focused on

your team gaining control of the match that the actual event is a blur. I'm not sure how much you actually enjoy those games when it is end to end, one team winning, then the other.

I've managed games like that and it's the same. Like when I took Tottenham to Arsenal in 2008 and came back with a 4–4 draw. A classic match but did I enjoy it? Only at the end. There was a point in the match, when we were 4–2 down, and I am thinking, we might get done six or seven here, and you are stood there dreading the fallout. We then rally, and score a couple of late goals, our end of travelling fans are going mad, and it's one of the most enjoyable nights I had at the club. It's very fine margins.

I think that's what made that game against Newcastle so good was that it could have gone either way and, at the time, there was a genuine title challenge still on. It was the perfect storm. Both teams are desperate to win the match, both teams only know how to play front-foot, attacking football, the floodlights are on, which always adds to the occasion, and it's Anfield. With hindsight, there was very little surprise that mad things went on that night.

We had a good team. Three at the back, very energetic wing-backs in Rob Jones and Jason McAteer, and in Steve McManaman, the perfect player to build the whole

system around; Stan Collymore able to be direct but also hit the wings; and Robbie Fowler, just a genius of a striker inside and outside of the box.

Newcastle, too. They had been magnificent that season. The attacking talent they had. Peter Beardsley, David Ginola, Les Ferdinand, they get Faustino Asprilla in – it was scary and we went into the game knowing that we had to go full out to attack them. Simple as that. We did that and what followed was pure chaos.

We get off to a great start, what a great cross by Stan and a typical header by Robbie, but then Newcastle come at us and – and this was the problem with our team – there were gaps and we were prone to let in silly goals. We're 2–1 down at half-time.

I was in midfield with John Barnes. We were facing David Batty and Rob Lee, two players with loads of energy. The midfield was a strange place to be that night. A lot of the play was in wide areas and the Anfield pitch wasn't very good. The central areas were cutting up, but we constantly played from the back and it was up to me and John to get the ball off our defenders. Not that easy with the ball bobbling up and David Batty introducing himself to your ankles.

It was all about risk and reward. For both teams. They really knew only one way, and that was to get on the ball and look forward for the creative guys. High wing-backs and full-backs, spaces in behind, let's have a go.

Second half and that's exactly what we did. Macca and Robbie combine brilliantly as ever to make it 2–2 but then we fall asleep again and Asprilla beats a dodgy offside trap, chips David James and we're losing again. Heads don't drop, though, the Anfield crowd won't allow for that, and from a delicious McAteer cross, Stan makes it 3–3. There's twenty-odd minutes left and it's 3–3!

Somehow, into injury time and it's still a deadlock. It wasn't for the want of trying. A draw suited no one, especially the supporters there that night who continued to push us forward. James made some saves in our goal to prevent a defeat, but it was the older heads, Barnsie and Rushie (who had come on as a sub) who played what seemed like seven one–twos before Barnes played Stan in, and on his very good left foot, he fires in the winner. Unbelievable. Iconic.

The crazy thing is, we did it all again the following season. Actually, it was a very different game in 1997. We battered them first half and were 3–0 up at the break. I'd say that first half was the best I felt in a Liverpool shirt. We were brilliant that night. Our movement, our finishing. Robbie, Macca, Paddy Berger, Barnsie still doing it.

We managed to throw away the lead, but what a winner from Robbie right at the end. A bullet header. One of the best winners I've ever seen. So brave. At the Kop end too. That is probably the more enjoyable game for me, but

because of what was at stake, the 1996 fixture remains more memorable. You had to feel a bit sorry for Kevin Keegan didn't you?

The images of him with his head in his hands after Collymore's strike, they are as iconic as anything that was served up on the pitch. Yes, you had to feel desperately sad for him. His team were rocking for half the season, playing the most attractive, attacking football we'd seen in a long time. Flying wingers, big Les at centre-forward, little Peter Beardsley dropping into pockets; a fabulous footballer, and they deservedly had a – what was it – eleven-point lead at one point?

Actually, Liverpool's win against Newcastle that night helped me lose a few quid. There was this Italian restaurant called Bruno's in Wanstead, east London. I was manager at West Ham by now, Frank Lampard Snr was my assistant, and he and I would often get in there with our wives after a game on a Saturday night. The owner there, Bruno, he liked a glass of wine and he loved his football, a great lad, and he would come over and chat to us about what was going on.

So, after Christmas, Newcastle have that massive lead over Manchester United, and he starts saying, there is no way that Kevin's team win this league.

'But Bruno, they are eleven points ahead, they're playing great, I can't see them losing it now.'

'No, no,' he says. 'Harry, they are useless, I will bet you two grand that Newcastle not win this league.'

I'm flabbergasted, but he's so confident.

'You take the bet with me, Harry?'

I'm telling him to get to the bookies if he is so sure, he'll get ten-to-one, but he only wants to bet with me. In the end, it felt rude to turn him down, so we make the bet, and that night at Anfield, as I watch Jamie and the Liverpool lads and crowd celebrate that most remarkable of wins, as much as I am pleased for Jamie and everyone, I'm thinking, that Italian dinner is going to be the most expensive of my life. Newcastle ended up runners-up to United with Liverpool third.

There seems to be something about Dad and strange bets in Italian restaurants. What about the lifetime of pizzas offered to the Bournemouth keeper if he kept a clean sheet against Manchester United when they came to Bournemouth in the FA Cup in 1984?

Bournemouth drawing Manchester United in the FA Cup was the biggest thing to happen to the club in years, and it certainly was the classic match of my time there. What a mad one. We were a struggling, then Third Division club, fighting off relegation, and Manchester United, the cup holders, are coming to Dean Court. It was a magic occasion and one we relished.

I wanted to make it special for the lads. Some managers will say they try to keep things normal for the really big matches, but I wanted to make it memorable. Why not? How often do the likes of Bryan Robson, the England captain, come to your place, or Ray Wilkins, or Arnold Mühren? We went for a good walk on the beach, like we used to do with West Ham on such occasions, and then for something to eat at the nearby popular Italian and pizzeria.

We had a keeper, Ian Leigh. We called him Nipper. He was a bit overweight. When I say a bit, I mean about 10 kg overweight. That night, the owner of the restaurant enthusiastically said to Nipper, keep a clean sheet and it's free pizzas for life. Nipper looked unusually focused, but we're all thinking, they've got Norman Whiteside and Frank Stapleton up front. We'll give it a good go, but even the biggest Bournemouth fan wouldn't have thought that Nipper was set for a lifetime of free pizzas.

It all felt so different. This was a small club. Great support but all very local, all very contained, and suddenly the spotlight was on us. I was getting on with being a young football manager, and on the press side of things, that involved a couple of local journalists that I got to know well. This was, of course, different, this was the big boys, national television interest, and I was facing big Ron Atkinson, a manager very used to the limelight. A manager who knew his way around an interview. I was still very much learning.

It had hardly been a glamorous run to the third round. We had a proper test at Windsor & Eton in the second round. Hung on at their place by the skin of our teeth for a goalless draw and scraped through at our place.

I have to admit, I didn't give Bournemouth much hope against United. Dad always had good footballing teams down there but, and with no disrespect, this one wasn't one of his best. Part of me was more interested in the opposition. I had the likes of Robson and Wilkins on my bedroom walls so I was excited to see them up close. I remember the tight little entrance at Dean Court. The team bus would park up, and the opposition would make their way in, in single file, into the even tighter away dressing room.

Suddenly there were these superstars in front of me. They seemed bigger, great hair, classy Adidas tracksuits, bit of expensive jewellery. International footballers. I'd love to say that I was fully behind Dad, but it was a thrill to see these guys, and if I am honest, I feared that it could be become very difficult for Dad's team.

Later, when I played in a few games that meant going away to the smaller clubs, you have to be at it. Whatever the conditions. Most grounds these days have very good pitches, and back then Bournemouth's wasn't the worst. There was one groundsman, John. He never stopped telling stories but sometimes he'd get around to seeing to

the surface and the pitch was OK. Nowadays there are more ground staff than supporters!

John was a real character, and the pitch wasn't the worst United's players would have played on. We had to rely purely on our workrate to beat them. Our form, though, didn't suggest that even on a quagmire of a pitch United had much to worry about. Not many would have backed us.

I was a realist, but with that, I knew football, I knew the FA Cup, and I knew that if we made it difficult for them, they could have an off-day, and something crazy might happen. Get in their faces, that was the key. Try to play our football, but play the channels, win setpieces, don't let them settle into any sort of rhythm, and that's exactly what happened. The boys were magnificent.

I remember hearing about some mind games, and that Dad had gone into his dressing room and told the lads that United didn't fancy it, that he'd heard that some of them were still in their tracksuits, watching some horse racing on *Grandstand* in the boardroom. Dad was going on about how easy they were taking it, and that was the proof. I'm sure Dad only knew they were watching the horses because he was too.

A few of them had been in the directors' room, still in their tracksuits, not long after two o'clock, watching

Grandstand's coverage of some race. I couldn't say if I was in there too, but I did go back to our dressing room and tell the lads that they were taking this game too lightly and we had a chance. You have to use any little advantage you can think of.

I remember watching the first half, and mostly watching Bryan Robson. Bournemouth were very organised, but Dean Court was never the most uncomfortable of grounds. They were a nice set of fans, polite, and so United's superstars weren't going to have their rhythm disrupted by a vocal and intimidating home crowd. 'Come on you Cherries!' It's hardly Millwall is it?

The game was tight, the lads working their socks off, and into the second half, still goalless, I felt our players were unsettling their superstars. Bryan Robson wasn't looking comfortable and like so many giant killings we took advantage of two setpieces and two mistakes by big-name players. First, Gary Bailey in their goal dropped a corner and Milton Graham buried it, and then two minutes later, Robson of all people dwelled on the ball, was robbed and Ian Thompson put us two up.

It was mayhem. Jubilation. I loved coaching and managing a small club like Bournemouth. I liked having to make deals, buy cheap and sell on for good money. After that win there was more press interest. I think I said that it was the greatest day of my life and the players' too, but it really was down to their efforts on the day. It must have given me a lot of confidence moving forward but I certainly wasn't suddenly impatient to start working in the top division after that. In fact, I had another eight very enjoyable years at Bournemouth, learning more and more about the art of managing.

It was bedlam in the stands. The crowd went crazy, and I just remember seeing Dad on the sidelines, celebrating wildly, and feeling so proud. Suddenly the posters on my walls meant nothing. It was all about him, it was all about Bournemouth.

I remember the days after the victory. *Good Morning Britain* brought their cameras to our house and filmed Mark and me eating our breakfast cereal. Surreal. What I remember was telling the producer that I loved Roland Rat, and he said he would send me a Roland Rat toy. If that producer is reading this, I still haven't received it.

As I say, I was very proud of Dad. I never really said much at school about it. If Bournemouth lost a game, you could hear nasty things being said in the playground. Now that the team had won a massive game, I wasn't going to say too much. I liked to keep a low profile.

It was a great time, but as I said immediately after the match, it was all about the players, and one of them,

Nipper, was in for a lifetime of pizzas. He must have got them for a bit, but not long as a new owner bought that pizzeria and stopped giving them away. That new owner's name was Harry Redknapp. A bit mean perhaps, but as his manager, I wasn't going to let my keeper pig out on pizzas was I?

Dad went on to have a lot of great results against Manchester United in the FA Cup, but I always loved hearing him and Pops talk about the day Dad's already mentioned when they saw Matt Busby's team at Highbury in February 1958, a match that turned out to be that brilliant young side's last in England before their tragic air crash.

That day and that match would have been memorable anyway. They were such a good team, full of wonderful young talent, and the match itself against the Arsenal was one of the best I have ever seen.

Dad took me along. Arsenal were our team and it was exciting to see the Busby Babes in town. We stood in our usual spot at the top left-hand corner of the North Bank, Dad with his flask of tea and a couple of sandwiches. He was an Arsenal fan, but there was also that excitement in the fact that a special team had come to the ground, a young team pushing for honours in Europe. That competition felt so new, Matt's team felt so new, so being just a young kid, it wasn't like an everyday Saturday at the match.

United were in their white away kit, Arsenal in their famous red and white tops. I was only eleven but I remember United coming out the blocks and smashing Arsenal. They battered them, taking a 3–0 half-time lead. Even the Arsenal fans were impressed, as people understood that they were witnessing something special.

To be fair to Arsenal, they came out for the second half and had a right go back, even drawing level, but you just felt that United's youngsters could go up a level, and they won the game 5–4. It was incredible. At the end of the game, as the players shook hands, the whole of Highbury applauded. Those in the posh seats stood up, and for a good five or ten minutes applause rang out into the cold north London air.

We were clapping the spectacle we'd witnessed, we were clapping Arsenal's effort to make a game of it, we were clapping raw, youthful talent, and we were clapping one of the truly great football teams this country has ever seen. Little did we know that this country would never see them again. A week later, so many of them were dead, and everyone there that day, for that amazing match, must have felt a deep and real sorrow for those young men who lost their lives.

Results like 5–4 were quite common back then, but the game was beginning to ever so slightly change. We were going from the WM formation and essentially five forwards to something, not yet defensive but more considered. The Busby Babes, though, were all about youthful vigour and forward movement. That's what I remember about that game at Highbury, just this sense of constant attack. It was attacking but it felt modern.

When it comes to matches that changed the way us English fans looked at the game, the year that stands out is 1953. Two iconic games at Wembley happened that year. One was the FA Cup final. Blackpool beat Bolton 4–3 in a match known for evermore as 'The Matthews Final'. You have to feel sorry for Stan Mortensen who scored a hat-trick that day, but there you go.

The game was old fashioned in the sense that Stanley Matthews would receive the ball, the full-backs, never crossing the halfway line, would wait and wait before jockeying him twenty-five yards from goal, he would draw them in, drop a shoulder and invariably beat them to their left and cross the ball in to a grateful centre-forward, in this case Mortensen.

Tactics and outlooks were changing, though, and no game proved that more than when the brilliant Hungary side came to Wembley, also in 1953 and Ferenc Puskás and Nándor Hidegkuti and József Bozsik pointed out to us English that not only were we no longer the perceived giants of the game, but tactics were very much moving on.

Suddenly the game was far more international. Matt Busby got that, that's why he pushed so hard to enter his club into the new European Cup competition. The old WM formation, static full-backs, stopper centre-halves, it was all beginning to change and a new wave of foreign superstar teams were playing matches that only underlined how quickly that change was happening.

Take the 1960 European Cup final, played at Hampden Park in Glasgow in front of what must have been 500,000 because everyone seems to say they were there. Real Madrid slaughtered Eintracht Frankfurt 7–3. Puskás was once again involved, scoring four, whilst Alfredo Di Stéfano (arguably the greatest player anyone had seen up to that point) got the other three goals.

The patterns they made on the pitch that evening, the way every player was involved, the skill levels; I remember seeing footage of it as a kid, and it changing the way we all thought about football. We sort of fell even deeper in love.

I had that feeling in 1982, watching the World Cup, and especially the game between Brazil and Italy in Barcelona. Brazil had blown us all away in the group stages, battering Scotland along the way, and their superstar footballers just seemed so exotic and new. I remember putting the television on that afternoon to watch the game, in which Brazil only needed a draw to progress to the semi-final.

Brazil settling for a draw? That Brazil? Don't make me laugh. The game was amazing. Zico, Sócrates, Éder, Oscar, that yellow kit. They played the game like I had never seen before. It was so off-the-cuff. Unscripted. It all seemed so different to games on *Match of the Day*. The bright colours. Yellow and blues. The heat of the Spanish summer. John Motson's crackling voice on the commentary.

The game also taught me that sometimes the very best do not win, and that sheer grit and organisation, plus a deadly centre-forward, can win football matches. Italy scored through Paolo Rossi, Sócrates equalised beautifully. Rossi scores again, another wonderful equaliser through Falcão. Brazil had their draw, but did they stop attacking, did they sit on the result? Of course they didn't. They didn't know how. Instead it was relentless flair. That's the best way to describe it, and in the end a late Rossi goal for his hat-trick meant they, the great Brazil team of 1982, were going home. I was only just nine years old, but I had my first taste of footballing heartbreak.

What a team they were, and what a match that was. That side were the closest we'd seen to their great 1970 side – the best of all time in my opinion, and I base that on another game they played against Italy. The 1970 World Cup final in Mexico City was against a very good Italian side, but it was an exhibition: 4–1. The football they played, the goals they scored, the individuals they had who came together as this magical team . . . It was a match that stayed with us all. I'm still not sure that performance has ever been bettered.

I remember hearing so much about that game and watching footage. I couldn't watch that last goal by Carlos Alberto enough. I still can't, to be fair. Talking of finals, when I was a boy, the match to watch was the cup final. The FA Cup final. The first one I remember, we were actually there. It was 1980. Uncle Frank was playing for West Ham against Arsenal. Mark was a big Hammers fan. I wasn't but I did like their players: Trevor Brooking, who scored the winner that day, I loved how he let the ball run across his body, and Alan Devonshire, so stylish. What I remember about the day was the colour. Walking up Wembley Way, the fans, the kits, West Ham's white away kit and Arsenal's bright yellow. It was a great day. To see my uncle lift the FA Cup. I think it was another occasion that told me that I had to be a footballer.

I think the FA Cup has done the same to loads of kids. It is special. One of my most fond memories of a game (or games) actually comes from that FA Youth Cup final I mentioned earlier. It was 1963. I was just sixteen years old, doing well, and our team made the final with the backing of the first team manager, Ron Greenwood. Ron was at every single Youth Cup tie; he loved the idea of the club's boys being just as vital as the first team. We went into the two-legged final against Liverpool knowing that he and his first-team players were all interested in us and how we got on. That's how it was back then. There was a real connection between the youth players and the senior lads.

Fifteen thousand Liverpool fans were also interested enough to come to the first leg at Anfield, and they saw their team win 3–1. They were captained by Tommy Smith, a player clearly destined for great things, and we travelled south gutted, thinking that we'd blown it.

The second leg saw another healthy crowd at Upton Park. It was a Saturday, an evening kick-off just hours after that year's senior FA Cup final. Manchester United had beaten Leicester. No one seemed too bothered in Wembley on this occasion, but at half-time at Upton Park, we were losing 2–1, and 5–2 down on aggregate with forty-five minutes to go. It didn't look good, but for some reason we came out and we just got at them. We battered them. Pace, aggression, the crowd slowly more and more behind us, we drove into Liverpool and their lead diminished. Tommy Smith was at centre-half that night, and our centre-forward, a boy called Martin Britt, terrorised him. I say 'boy', Martin was a man at fifteen, and we were throwing crosses in, me from one wing, John

Sissons from the other, and Martin headed in four goals that night, helping us to a 6–5 victory.

Ron Greenwood was ecstatic, I saw him crying with joy. He knew what it meant for the club's future, and ten of that eleven went on to play first-team football at West Ham. Even now, it's one of my most memorable matches.

As a manager, I had more great moments in the cup, and the final in 2008 when we won with Portsmouth has to stand out as one of my favourite matches. I loved my time at Pompey, and we built a great, great side. David James, Sol Campbell, Lassana Diarra, Niko Kranjčar, so many good internationals bought on a shoestring budget. Nwankwo Kanu. I got him for nothing. A simple phone call. We had no strikers and I heard he was a free agent. 'Are you fit?' I asked him.

'Yes, boss, I went for a run yesterday.'

That'll do me. My coaches thought I was mad, but he came in and immediately impressed. He was great for us and scored the winner at Wembley that day.

The most memorable win on the way to Wembley was the 1–0 victory at Old Trafford. What a team they had. They won the Champions League that season. We played great and got a late penalty. The final was different. We were playing Cardiff from the Championship and this time we were the favourites.

With that, I sensed the lads were nervous and it was actually a night out on the Friday, a karaoke machine and the best Elvis impression I have ever seen from Hermann Hreiðarsson that settled everyone down and we were able to go out, relaxed, be professional and win.

It's right up there with my most memorable moments as a manager but I cherish games I had with Bournemouth in the lower leagues just as much. Winning promotion to the second tier in 1987 was some achievement, as was winning the Associate Members Cup in 1984. I loved the everyday nature of football management and to see my Bournemouth side win a trophy of any sort was terrific. I knew what went into keeping the club going, the work that we all put in, not for glory but for the love of the club and the people.

The game was actually supposed to be played at Wembley but the Horse of the Year Show had ruined the turf there so we tossed a coin, Hull won, and the final was played up there. Hull had a decent side. Steve McLaren played, but it was their centre-forward that we had to watch out for. Billy Whitehurst put the fear of God into most pros that he faced. He was a huge brute of a man. Let's just say he loved the physical side of the game. In the opening minutes, he went up for a corner and took out my keeper and two defenders. Wallop! All three of them are spark out on the floor. We looked down and out too, losing 1–0 but the team rallied and we won the game 2–1. It was a special night, and we had the best party on the coach home afterwards.

I so wanted to go to that final in Hull. It was a school night and Mum and Dad said I couldn't. I was miserable for ages. Especially with the team winning and knowing I'd missed out on seeing them lift a trophy.

I actually made my first-team debut against Hull a few years later. Billy Whitehurst played then too. I was sixteen, we were at their place, and I was sub. The team were brilliant that day and took a four-goal lead. Dad turns to me. 'Get warm, Jamie, you're going on.' This is my moment.

Billy had caught my eye throughout the game. I loved the skilful players, Hoddle, Zico, Ruud Gullit, but I was transfixed with Billy. I'm sure he was a fine centre-forward, but it was his sheer physicality and attitude that got me that day. Six feet four, broad shoulders, a face that had been in more than the odd tear-up, and with us winning and winning well, he was looking for another one. He's snarling, he looks like a club bouncer looking for drunks to beat up, and as Dad put me on, Billy is an angry bomb ready to go off.

'Be careful with him, son,' were Dad's quiet words of encouragement. Billy must have seen me, a kid, the opposing manager's kid, and thought, that'll do me. The ball is played into my feet, my first touch in pro-football, what a moment. It's under control. So far, so good. But then I hear him. Coming from behind me is Billy and he's growling, he's on the hunt. I can't even explain the noise. Graaaaggghhhullllll! Something like that.

Thrown by the sound, I rush things, and quickly pass it out to the left-back, a great lad called Paul Burrell. In all the stress, I leave the pass a bit short, and Billy is on his way. Paul is a big lad, he could handle himself, and he gets to the ball first, but Billy doesn't care about trivial matters like that and goes right through him, hurtling Paul into the air. Paul gets up, squares up to Billy, who simply lifts him by the neck of his shirt and holds him up. Everyone is in, a nineteen-man brawl, only the two keepers and myself, the kid who started the whole thing, are watching on. I think our lot decided quickly that it was a fight not worth having. They had Billy Whitehurst. We weren't going to win.

I also remember a memorable match the following season. I had played more games, and we took on Chester. They had a lad Dad's already mentioned called Graham Barrow. Big Lancastrian midfielder. Nice bloke but he was trying to kick lumps out of me. Muddy pitch and this guy is right on me. But, for ninety minutes, I got on the ball, I was playing, passing well, avoiding his tackles, and it was a match when I thought, you know what, I can do this, I'm ready. I agreed to sign for Liverpool very soon after.

Most memorable games take you to very happy places but some remind us of harder times. I think of the 1990

World Cup in Italy, just before I signed for Liverpool, a joyous, iconic summer of football but a very trying time for Dad and the family.

I remember being at home, excited, knowing that Dad was out at the World Cup with his great friend and Bournemouth's chief executive, Brian Tiler. Brian and Dad were very close, worked very well together and our families all got along. It was a thrill knowing that they were out in Italy, watching the games I was seeing on the television. Dad would ring Mum every night, but after the quarter-final match in Rome that saw Italy beat Ireland, when no phone call came, Mum knew something wasn't right.

The next morning, beside herself with worry, she took the call. It was from the Bournemouth chairman. 'There's been a car accident, Sandra. Brian is dead. Harry is doing OK, they've had to put him in a coma.' Brian had been killed when the car was hit head on when travelling on a duel carriageway near the Italian capital.

We were in bits. What does 'OK' mean? People have died, Dad is in a coma. How 'OK' is he? Mum, Mark and I went straight out to Rome, and I remember walking into this Roman hospital, these huge ceilings, and there he is, Dad, in bed. My hero. He was awake by now but in a bad way. I couldn't handle it, and I collapsed. I fainted. I came to with a wet flannel on my head. I think Dad was more worried about me than he was about himself.

It was a hard time. I was lying in that bed, so sad for Brian and his wife, Hazel, and their daughter, Michelle. My injuries were bad, apparently medics on the scene presumed that I was dead and I had a sheet placed over my face. My skull injuries were a big concern, but with the right care I made a full recovery. In Rome, I was worried about Jamie and Mark and, of course, Sandra. I didn't want them worrying, and with Jamie and Mark, I could talk about the matches at the World Cup, just so we all felt normal.

The iconic game was the England v. West Germany semi-final. I think Mark and I watched it in a local café, in Rome. I had been blown away by Gazza's form, but as great as that match was, it passed me by. I was watching, but my mind was on Dad, in the hospital. England were out but Dad had tickets for the final – tickets he and Brian were meant to use, tickets that he gave to my brother and me.

That was a strange occasion. The Germans won against Argentina, but it was not a memorable match at all, and it felt strange for us boys to be there, to be in Dad and Brian's seats. It was a very emotional time that summer and the backdrop was the World Cup. A World Cup that continues to evoke so many memories.

The thing is, Italy seemed to be the footballing mecca at the time. All the great players were in Serie A, the World Cup was there and, in AC Milan, they had the best club

Harry: A young Jamie was a constant companion to me while I was managing Bournemouth. It wouldn't be long before he was playing in the first team.

Jamie: The King! I only worked for five weeks under Kenny Dalglish at Liverpool, but he remains an inspirational figure in my career.

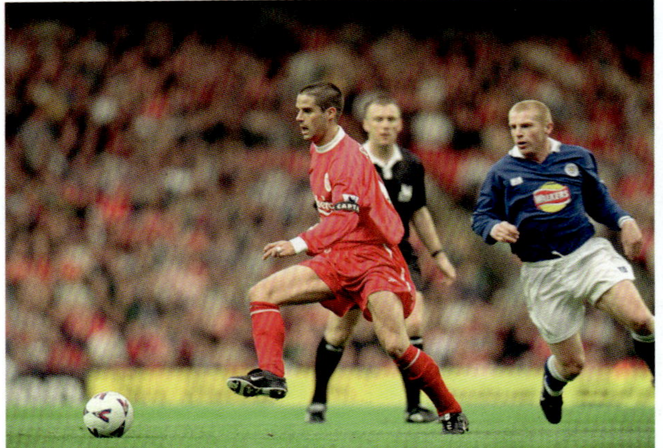

Jamie: When Gérard Houllier made me captain of Liverpool in 1999, it was one of the proudest moments of my career. *(Clive Brunskill/Allsport)*

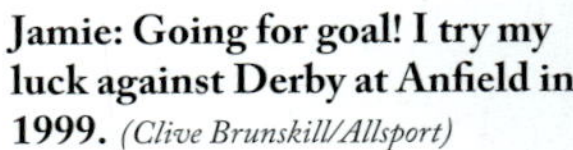

Jamie: Going for goal! I try my luck against Derby at Anfield in 1999. *(Clive Brunskill/Allsport)*

Jamie: Get in there! My last ever goal for Liverpool against Charlton in October 2001. *(Ben Radford/Allsport)*

Harry: Nothing better than working with the players. I put the Portsmouth lads through their paces. *(MIKE WALKER/Alamy Stock Photo)*

Harry: Play up Pompey! Winning the FA Cup in 2008 was one of the best days of my career. *(Colorsport/Andrew Cowie)*

Harry: Kevin Bond (left) played under me at Bournemouth and was a trusted assistant at several clubs, including here at Southampton in 2005. *(Colorsport)*

Harry: The North London derby in 2008 proved to be one of the most memorable of the Premier League era when we [Tottenham] came from 3–1 and 4–2 behind to draw 4–4. *(CHRIS RATCLIFFE/AFP via Getty Images)*

Jamie: I fend off Newcastle's Rob Lee in a match at Anfield in 1996 that is still regarded the Premier League's finest. Liverpool won 4–3. *(Allsport UK/Allsport)*

amie: Gazza told me that he was going to mimic the infamous 'Dentist Chair' if he scored against Scotland at Wembley during the 1996 European Championships. As usual, he didn't disappoint… *(Photo by Stu Forster via Getty Images)*

amie: Making a difference. I came on against Scotland during the European Championships in 1996 and helped England to a 2–0 win. Sadly, a late injury that day meant it was the end of my tournament. *(Photo by Daniel Bardou/Onze/Icon Sport)*

Jamie: Still the boss! I finished my career at Southampton with Dad and we celebrated this 2–0 win over my former club, Liverpool, in January 2005.

Harry: The best of enemies Jamie plays for England against my Rest of the World team in the 2018 Soccer Aid match at Old Trafford. England won on penalties.

Iarry: Only golf comes
lose to matching our
ɔve of football. It was
pleasure for us both
ɔ meet Tiger Woods at
. P. MacManus's golf
ay in Ireland.

Harry: I'm the King of the Jungle! Winning *I'm a Celebrity…Get me Out of Here!* in 2018. *(James Gourley/ITV/Shutterstock)*

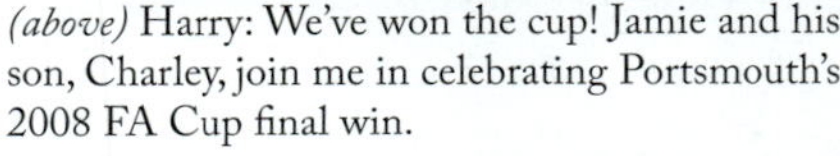

(above) Harry: We've won the cup! Jamie and his son, Charley, join me in celebrating Portsmouth's 2008 FA Cup final win.

(right) **Jamie: It's a young man's game. I watch from the sidelines as my son Beau plays for Brentford's youth team against Bournemouth in 2024.** *(Leo Moynihan)*

(below) The best of friends!

team around. I remember watching the 1989 European Cup final, and salivating as their team, with Marco van Basten, Gullit, Frank Rijkaard, Paolo Maldini and Franco Baresi took Steaua Bucharest apart, 4–0. European Cup finals aren't usually that one-sided, but most teams aren't usually that AC Milan side, are they?

It's a great competition. The European Cup, the Champions League. It's given us so many great matches. The finals are great spectacles and so often they have been tight, but they are always special. The one that stands out for me is the 1968 final at Wembley that saw Matt Busby lift the trophy. Ten years after the Munich air crash, ten years after I stood and watched his young side at Highbury, and now, with a new team full of superstars, they were crowned European Champions.

I love that football gives us those moments. I won't lie, though, I was less pleased with Manchester United's Champions League win in 1999. I have nothing against United really, and usually I'd want the English club to do well, but as a Liverpool player you soon learn from your surroundings and that, I'm afraid, means wanting United to lose.

I was actually on my way to a holiday with my then wife. We were getting on a plane to France, and I heard that Bayern Munich were 1–0 up. That'll do. We get to

our hotel, I put the television on, and United have won 2–1. That's the holiday ruined.

It was also strange the night in 2005 when Liverpool won the same competition in Istanbul. I had finished at Southampton that season, and my knee was in bits. I wanted to play another season somewhere but I was in pain, and I flew to Colorado to see the late, great Dr Richard Steadman, the Lionel Messi of orthopaedic surgeons. It was the day of the final, I had surgery so he could take a look inside, and I was in recovery feeling very woozy from all the medication.

Dr Steadman came in to my room, and I have the final on. It's the first half. AC Milan are dismantling Liverpool. He tells me the news. The knee is bad and, if I tried to play on, I'd need a new one very soon. AC Milan go three up. I am in tears. The nurses might have been thinking I'm sad about Liverpool, which I am, but the tears are mainly because my career is over. In Istanbul, my old mate Carra, as he walks off at half-time, might be thinking the same thing.

I then doze off, the drugs still doing their thing, and when I wake up, it's 3–3. I am sure that it is the effects of all the drugs in my system. I am having some sort of crazy trip – 3–3? It can't be.

The game was a miracle. Clubs like Liverpool, far from a great team that year, can produce moments of pure magic.

For that, a lot of credit has to go to Steven Gerrard. I remember the first time Dad saw him play. A Merseyside derby at Anfield in 1999. Always a great occasion. Dad always had a good eye for a player. He'd come to see me, but after the game all he wanted to talk about was Stevie, who had come on and played at right-back, making two crucial clearances to ensure us the three points. 'Cor, he's some player, that kid, Gerrard,' Dad said. 'But he ain't a right-back. That boy will play in midfield.' It's as if Dad knows football!

How about games today? It seems to me that the matches have got very tactical, and the great games have been as much about the managers and their tactics as they are the players. Klopp's Liverpool v. Pep's Manchester City. They were so good to watch, but very technical.

I agree. Where is all the flair, where are the spontaneous moments in matches, where are the end-to-end games, with defensive mistakes and loads of goals? You certainly don't get many 4–3s or 5–4s any more do you? We can look back, though, and be at the great games can't we? You never forget them. You never forget getting on a bus with your dad, the sights, the smells, the people. Let's hope there's plenty more soon.

Chapter 8

Proper Hard Men

JAMIE

I have two words. Billy & Whitehurst. I was lucky enough (or unlucky enough, depending what mood I am in) to play in an era when the rules still allowed for a certain degree of roughhouse tactics, and tackles were still just about on the harmful side of grievous bodily harm. Plenty of players in the 1980s and 1990s would hope to be named the hardest man in English football, but unless they are called Billy Whitehurst, they would be kidding themselves.

Vinnie Jones, for good reasons that much-lauded tough guy of our game, was once in a room with his Sheffield United teammates, and when asked 'Who is the hardest man in the game?' he paused, pointed at Billy and said, 'You'd better ask him.'

My first foray on to a first-team Football League pitch saw me immediately rattled by Billy's presence, and that poor pass I gave to Paul Burrell because of his grunting behind me sparked a riot. Well, it looked like a riot to me. To Billy it was probably a mere warm-up to his Saturday night.

Born in South Yorkshire, Billy started his career as a semi-professional, working as a bricklayer. Rumour has it the bricks were scared of him. He went on to become a cult goalscorer at numerous clubs, including Hull where I faced him, Sheffield United and Newcastle. Stories of bar-room brawls, bare-knuckle fighting and a taste for the blood of central defenders gave him a kind of cult status among players. I remember hearing that Martin Keown, no choirboy himself, was asked about Billy and said he only played against him once, 'But once was enough.'

I would listen intently to Alan 'Jockey' Hansen when I arrived at Anfield, and he made me laugh with a story about an afternoon when Liverpool turned up at Oxford in the late 1980s. Billy was playing for the then Manor Ground club, but Jockey and his centre-half partner, Mark Lawrenson, were given the fantastic news that Billy, a player they both had had run-ins with in the past, was not playing. For Jockey and Lawro, it was like being told they had won the pools.

The rumour was that Billy had got involved in some sort of misunderstanding that had turned into a brawl that had turned into a mini-riot, and the cuts that he had to his face were too severe to allow him to play. Neither Jockey or Lawro were the type to wish ill of anyone, but not worrying about the centre-forward's famous elbows might just make their work that afternoon a bit easier and far more enjoyable.

The two defenders got their kit on with a spring in their step, went out to the tunnel to get out on to the pitch and to their joint horror there, in his full yellow Oxford kit, was Billy Whitehurst. To add to their sense of fear, the cuts on his face had been coarsely sewn up with twenty stitches and a few staples for good measure. Billy looked over at these European Cup-winning, cultured defenders, smiled and said, 'Afternoon, Alan. Afternoon, Mark.' Gulp. Frankenstein's Monster might have found a kindred spirit that day, and for Jockey and Lawro, the afternoon had taken a turn for the worse. Two hours later they would have the bruises to prove it.

HARRY

Billy certainly came with a reputation. Don't get me wrong, he was a good centre-forward, strong as an ox, good in the air, but it was his ability to get 'stuck in' that had many defenders in no doubt that the game would get physical.

That time when Billy took out three of my Bournemouth players in one go, we didn't have enough physios to cope!

I didn't know Billy well, but I could tell that his hard-man persona was not an act. Billy was just tough and was from a tough place – a mining village called Thurnscoe near Barnsley – so the way he was on a football pitch was very much him. Some who like to think of themselves as football tough guys aren't, and I think there's a big difference between hard and nasty.

We've all come across players who were just plain out of order, going over the top, trying to hurt people. I don't call that hard, it's cowardice. When I was going to matches as a young boy, the game still wasn't very dirty. Yes, players could bodycheck goalkeepers and of course it was physical, but those tactics that came in, in the 1960s, that saw players almost assaulting opponents were yet to rear their head.

The players I went to see in the 1950s, they were hard though. My God, they were tough. Tommy Docherty at Arsenal? He was made of granite at right-half. The great Tommy Banks, who played for Bolton and England, now he was hard. He played at left-back in the Bolton team that beat Manchester United in the 1958 FA Cup final, and went to the World Cup with England that summer. Big, strong, brave, no nonsense. A typical Lancastrian. As hard as Tommy was, it was always said that he was the nicest fella away from the pitch. Bobby Charlton certainly talked about how strong and how tough an opponent Tommy was.

If you were a winger facing Bolton back then, and you weren't getting the better of Tommy, you wouldn't bother trying to swap wings because at right-back you'd find Roy Hartle. Roy was tough, never dirty, but uncompromising in the tackle, and they both loved to torment wingers.

They weren't dirty though. The tackles might have shaken Bolton's ground to its rafters, but it was never dirty, never meant to hurt anyone. Crash, the tackle would come in, the winger was on the floor, and then there was an almost ironic enquiry into how the guy was before a hand was given out to help the poor bloke up. Roy was given the nickname 'Chopper' when Ron Harris was still a nipper in short trousers.

I used to like a guy over the Arsenal called Danny Clapton. A good winger. Ron Greenwood had been assistant manager at Arsenal before coming to West Ham, and used to tell me a funny story.

Arsenal took on and beat Bolton 6–1 one Saturday, and then were due up at Burnden Park on the following Wednesday. Danny Clapton had tormented Tommy Banks all afternoon at Highbury, words had been exchanged, and Tommy was heard saying to Danny, 'When you come to our place, you'll get gravel-rash.'

The return game up there gets started, and Tommy is getting involved with Danny, letting him know he was there, and so Danny, getting no joy, has an idea. He switches wings. No point. He goes over to the other side and Roy is no less charitable. Ron used to say that Tommy shouted across the pitch, ''Ere, Roy, when you're finished with him, kick him back this way will ya?'

David 'Bumble' Lloyd, the former England Test cricketer, television commentator and massive Bolton fan, also told a story about Tommy. The England team were facing Brazil in their second group game at the 1958 World Cup. Brazil had a fantastic side and would go on to win it, and before the game, at a team meeting, the England manager Walter Winterbottom said in his very posh voice, 'Now, Banks, tonight I want to you put Garrincha out of the game.'

Tommy paused, had a think and said, 'Mr Winterbottom, do you mean just for tonight, or permanently?'

What Billy Whitehurst would have made of Tommy Banks and Roy Hartle, I don't know. I would have thought there would be some sort of mutual respect between the three of them. There might be a few teeth on the floor, but a bit of respect after. Roy and Tommy could look after themselves, no doubt about it, but Billy is certainly right up there among the hardest of all time.

If Billy was that hard, I still don't understand why Dad sent me on to play my first ever game against him, when I was aged just sixteen. What's that all about? Where's the

duty of care? Mum would have killed Dad if anything had happened to her baby!

Lucky for him, I came out unscathed and it was actually those run-ins with the likes of Billy and other hard men in the third tier of English football that made me realise that even at sixteen, I was capable of (just about) handling myself. I also had some good guides at Bournemouth.

Jimmy Gabriel was Dad's assistant at the club – a former Scottish international and a great guy. Jimmy had played as a defensive midfielder and knew a thing or two about the dark arts. He could see that my game wasn't about all that but told me that, to make it, I would have to be able to look after myself. Dad, a skilful winger, had not been armed with much knowledge about all of that, so it was with Jimmy that I learned about rolling over the ball when challenging for it, to make contact with the guy out to hurt you. It was all about protection. 'If you don't, the other fella will,' Jimmy would say. 'If they go high, you go higher!'

It was exactly the education I was looking for, and confirmed to me that I was right to turn down Tottenham. It wasn't long before my education would continue in the top flight, and the teachers this time were the Crazy Gang.

Wimbledon came to Anfield in January 1991. I hadn't been at the club long, and Kenny Dalglish put me on the bench. I'm seventeen, it is a massive moment for me. I walk in from the bus, into Anfield, the hallowed ground, and then I hear the music coming from the away dressing room. Boom, boom, boom! John Fashanu is walking around, looking scary. The dressing room door is left wide open, and there he was, oiled up, only his shorts on, stretching in the doorway, doing all these martial arts poses, and he's a big, imposing lump. I've not seen anything like it before. Even the music is new. It's intimidating.

I was a kid, remember, and I'm sure the likes of Kenny himself, Steve McMahon and John Barnes were accustomed to it all. I always remembered Vinnie's early challenge on Steve McMahon in the 1988 FA Cup final. It was a whack. Today, that's the earliest red card of all time! McMahon does not flinch, in fact he gives Vinnie an elbow on the way down.

The Crazy Gang's game was always about intimidation and it was up to you to deal with it. They would try to win that battle in the tunnel. At Selhurst Park, where they played back then, the tunnel was tight and there was none of the polite acknowledgements you might get elsewhere. Other places, there might be a nod to someone you knew, a quick hand shake with an old teammate, but against Wimbledon it was different.

Wimbledon had some good, good footballers. John Scales came to us, Dennis Wise was a fantastic player, Warren Barton, Terry Phelan, all international footballers.

They were great athletes, they could play but they were tough, and they wanted to use their reputation to give them an advantage.

Chelsea came to Anfield in 1992. It was a tight game, physical. Chelsea had three of the former Crazy Gang in their line-up: Dave Beasant in goal, Dennis Wise and Vinnie Jones in midfield. We are struggling a bit, Chelsea have equalised in the second half, and late on, we have the ball out wide. I have made a run into the box, and Vinnie has gone in, crash, his elbow right into the side of my face. He's done my nose. As I get up, it's a bit blurry but I see Vinnie walking towards me, and he says, 'Try to run by me again, son, and I'll break your fucking legs.'

I never had a problem with Vinnie, that was just how he talked on the pitch, but OK, I think, it's going to be like that, is it? Last minute and I see my teammate Mark Walters going down the wing, and I think, fuck it, I need to be in that box. The only thing is, I have to run past Vinnie. I take a massive detour, but bust a gut to get in there, arrive at the back post, the ball breaks free, and I smash it in at the Kop end to win us the game. The feeling of pure euphoria is seemingly matched by a surge of testosterone, and as I am running back to the halfway line, I see Vinnie and I'm shouting, 'You fucking prick, you fucking want some d'ya? Let's fucking have it.'

Minutes later the final whistle went, and with the adrenaline slightly subsided, I am thinking, oh no, what

have I done? I can safely say that no one in the history of football has ever stayed out on the pitch as long as I did that day. All four corners of the ground got my applause. I was waiting until the away team's bus left.

To be fair to Vinnie, he was as good as gold about it after. That was the era. Yes, he elbowed me in the face, doing my nose, and yes I gave it back to him, but it was forgotten after. I do think that, today, there would have been uproar, days of social media and podcast scrutiny and the two players almost talked into some crappy feud. Back then, it was just done and dusted.

Most people in football will have a story about Wimbledon and the Crazy Gang. They had some tough guys in their team, and my first experience with them in the Premier League proved that even their chairman would try to wind them up to get them in the mood.

It was the first game of the season in 1993, West Ham's first in the Premier League. As Billy Bonds's assistant, I got to the ground early and the groundsman told me that the Wimbledon owner, Sam Hammam, was already in their dressing room, and he had a pile of pens with him. I didn't understand, but apparently Sam had been in there for almost an hour.

When I went in, I found the room covered in graffiti, and it's all about their players. Insults calling them all sorts. 'John Fashanu is a wanker!' 'Vinnie Jones is a prick!' That sort of thing. I couldn't believe it.

'What have you done?' I said to Sam.

'No, you lot have done it.'

As if we would write insults about people like Vinnie and Fash on the away dressing-room wall. It didn't make any sense, but there is the club chairman, standing in front of me and blatantly lying, and using these methods to apparently gee up his team. Sam felt that his lot would see it, think we'd written about them and they would be suitably fired up. Madness.

First of all, we had to cancel the regular tour given to kids that took them into the dressing rooms before games. No need for them to see that language, and then when Billy Bonds arrived I could see that he was visibly upset.

We'd only lost Bobby Moore a few months before and it did make you wonder where the game had gone from Mooro's time. I was actually offered the Bournemouth job again not long after that incident, and I would be lying if I said it didn't cross my mind to leave the top flight. Maybe we were upset about it because we had been brought up around Bobby Moore and the standards he set, and this seemed ugly. How had it come to a club chairman acting like that?

Funnily enough, there used to be an argument back when I was playing for West Ham that we were too nice, that we lacked a nasty streak. Back in 1967, we signed a centre-half from Celtic, a guy called John Cushley. John's first game was out in Germany on a pre-season tour against Borussia Dortmund. First half, and he was getting the run-around from a great German forward called Siggi Held. He had played in the 1966 World Cup final, and was taking out the memory of that defeat on us.

John had been murdered by Siggi, and when we came in at half-time, he was fuming. 'That's it, I've had enough!' he shouted. 'The next time that Held fella is on the ball, I am going to snap him in half. . .'

Ron Greenwood turned to him and said, 'Not in this team you won't,' and went on to give him a right rollocking for simply suggesting it. If he was going to get the better of him, he was going to do it fairly. That was the West Ham way.

Not that Bobby Moore couldn't handle himself; it was just that he never had to, so good was he at reading the game. It was an era of very tough players and teams, and I don't think many came tougher than Leeds. Don Revie's men were particularly adept at the dirty stuff, and on one occasion I bit.

It was 1968, and Leeds came to Upton Park to play us and, immediately, they were up to their tricks. Billy Bremner loved all that, and on three or four occasions, at throw-ins, he's standing on my feet. 'Billy, fuck off,' I say, but he carries on, stamping on them. I look to the ref, to the linesman, but nothing is being done, and so when he does it again, I snap and I give him a good boot. Some words are said to Billy and the officials, and I am told to go and take an early bath.

After a bit of argy-bargy, I'm going off and I have to walk past Mooro. To be fair to him, he knows what Leeds are all about and he just gives me a look and a shrug, as if to say, 'What can you do?'

I think players like Dad, the more skilful players in that era or even mine, they wouldn't be classed as hard, but they had to be brave, and that is a form of toughness. Take John Barnes. Barnsie was the bravest footballer I ever played with.

When he did his Achilles, John was told he might not play again, but he got back, and knowing he would never be that explosive winger, he simply took his game and shifted to being this clever, talented, holding midfielder who could make everything tick over. That meant getting on the ball, and that meant receiving it in certain places where he knew a severe tackle from behind was imminent. He never shied away. Not once. Constant availability.

It didn't matter how bad the game was going, if we were playing poorly, under pressure, John was there offering himself. When things are a bit tits up, the easiest thing to do is mark yourself out of the game. Go and stand near

someone, be out of range, subtle little movements away from the play. John never once hid.

What he had to his advantage was incredible ability and close control. John could offer himself to a full-back under pressure, with three around him, but we knew he was that good that he could control it, get it out, play it on, and we might be away. Now, John was a big lad and could look after himself, if needs be, but he was so classy that he'd either just draw the foul or evade the tackle.

I think Pep would have loved to have had him. That spot in front of the centre-backs is vital to his methods, and Rodri, like John, is so good in those tight situations. The thing is, though, what Rodri has that John didn't is far more protection from the referees and the rule book. He also has far better pitches.

Imagine these teams of today trying to play their intricate way out from the box, one–twos with the keeper, getting it to the midfielder with his back to goal, but with the ball bobbling up by his earholes, and someone with the tenacity of Dennis Wise keen to introduce himself to their ankles. The changes in the rules and the changes in pitch technology have made it so hard to compare the generations when it comes to ability but it's the same when measuring a player's toughness. John Barnes, though, he would be up there just for sheer bravery.

I look at Lionel Messi, and – while he had to put up with some rough stuff, especially at Barcelona when he faced two Real Madrid centre-backs, Sergio Ramos and Pepé, who were arguably the last of the really physical and perhaps 'dirty' defenders – it is clear he is not the same sort of fiery character as his compatriot, Diego Maradona.

Maradona, like Pelé, had to be hard. They had to give it back because it was about standing up for yourself. Pelé was kicked out of the 1966 World Cup, and similarly Maradona was kicked out of the 1982 clash with Italy by Claudio Gentile, the feared hard man from Juventus.

What about the fight after the Spanish Cup final when Maradona was at Barcelona in 1984? Barcelona were facing Athletic Bilbao, a team they had long had some battles with, but no one had seen anything like the brawl that went on out on the pitch that night. Maradona? If you thought he had moves with a football at his feet, you should look up him fighting as well. If he learned his footballing skills on the street, it is clear that he also learned to fight there, because he is throwing punches, elbows, knees, and all the while he's being attacked by a load of Basque country opponents – including the fearsome Andoni Goikoetxea – after his blood.

Jamie mentioned Claudio Gentile. I never saw much of him but he had some reputation. I went for dinner in Marbella years ago with Trevor Francis, Graeme Souness and our wives. Trevor and Graeme were playing out in Italy at the time, and Trevor was winding Graeme up saying that when they played Juventus, Graeme had bottled it against the Italian left-back. Graeme wasn't having it, of course, but even for Trevor to suggest that a player like Souness might think twice about having it with Gentile tells you how hard he must have been. Diego Maradona certainly found out.

When I think of modern hard men, I do think of Souness and Bryan Robson. Two colossal characters in the English game in the late 1970s and 1980s. Both were genuinely hard, tough guys. They would fly into tackles, they would stand up to any aggro a teammate might be getting and they would lead by example for both their clubs and their countries.

The biggest compliment I could give to either of them was that they reminded me of the great Dave Mackay. Bill Nicholson said he was the greatest Tottenham player of all time, Steve Perryman told me, and then Jimmy Greaves said the same, so that will do me. Dave was a fantastic player, he could do it all, but my word he was tough. Never dirty, but he would never shy away from a challenge, and you felt sorry for the bloke going up against him.

I love that iconic photo from 1966 of McKay, where he's got Billy Bremner up by the collar of his shirt. Billy looks like he doesn't fancy it and, to be fair to him, I don't blame him. One of my ex-teammates and Dad's old players who always fancied it was Neil 'Razor' Ruddock. Razor just

enjoyed all the aggro in a game. He genuinely loved it. It sometimes just made him laugh but, if it got serious, he was always on hand to get involved.

Putting Eric Cantona's collar down when we played Manchester United might have been a bit provocative but even a big man and personality like the Frenchman would think twice about having it with Razor.

Liverpool were never a dirty team; in fact, like Dad's West Ham side, we had many critics who suggested we weren't physical enough, hence why we signed Paul Ince in 1997. We did have players, though, who could quietly look after themselves. Ronnie Whelan, a lovely, unassuming Irishman, but when it came to it, he was as tough as I've seen. Ronnie didn't claim to be tough, he didn't covet a reputation for all that, but he would just quietly go about his business and any retribution would be carried out. A silent assassin.

We had Julian Dicks, like Razor and Incey another former Hammer, in the early 1990s as well. Less silent than Ronnie but no less deadly. Julian was known for his wild ways, his ferocious shot and his love of the game's bloodsports, but what we must also remember about Julian is that he had an absolute wand of a left foot. He could ping a ball about a pitch for fun, and if it's true that he also used it to decapitate wingers silly enough to try it on (on my full debut with Bournemouth I saw him kick a winger into West Ham's Chicken Run, part

of the East Stand, while wearing a knee brace – welcome to first-team football), he also had the talent that should have won him more international caps. Standing in his way was Stuart Pearce, another very hard player (what is it with left-backs?) but maybe he won more England recognition because he was able to control his aggression and never lost focus.

Dicks had played some football, prior to West Ham, at Birmingham, and I think I'm right in saying that the Midlands club had a few very hard men passing through in the 1980s: Julian, Mark Dennis, who loved a red card, Pat Van Den Hauwe, who loved a scrap, Noel Blake, an absolute beast of a centre-back, and up front Mick Harford . . . probably the only man who Billy Whitehurst might think twice about asking to step outside.

Mick Harford! Mick was so hard even the Crazy Gang left him alone. Wimbledon used to always have an initiation for new players. Cars would be damaged, clothes cut to shreds, all of that sort of thing. When Mick joined in 1994, all he got was a hello and a warm welcome.

Mick would stick his head in anywhere. He was far from dirty, he was just a classic old centre-forward whose job was to battle with the centre-backs, hold the ball up, bring others in and get on the end of things to score goals, even if that meant some harm to himself.

I remember hearing about one day when he got some of that harm from Sam Allardyce, himself a bit of a unit. Big Sam gave Mick a right whack with the elbow and cut his face to pieces. He smashed up his mouth, teeth came through his lip, his teeth were everywhere, and it took 100 stitches to clean it all up. It was said that the nurse doing the procedure cried, so severe were the injuries. As for Mick, he discharged himself from hospital the same day, and got back to training as soon as possible. I'm sure his next encounter with Sam was an interesting one.

Having said that, players like Mick Harford, the genuine hard ones, they don't seek out revenge or hold silly vendettas, like wannabe movie tough guys. These are footballers who just play with everything they have, give it their all. That can often mean it gets a bit brutal but then they are off, and it's on to the next one.

I mean, there are plenty of tough footballers who aren't necessarily genuinely hard away from the pitch. Norman Hunter at Leeds back in the 1960s and early 1970s had a bit of reputation. He got the nickname 'Bite yer Legs' but meeting him, he was the furthest thing from all that. Ron 'Chopper' Harris, his sometime nemesis at Chelsea, was a bit of a boy, a Hackney lad who liked the rough part of the game. I always thought Norman was different.

Leeds picked him up as a talented ball-playing defender, but it was drilled into him that, if he was going to make it in Don's team, he had to be more aggressive, learn how to give it. This was the most humble, nicest man you could meet, who didn't seem to have an aggressive bone in his body, but in time, while keeping that sweet left foot of his, he certainly learned whatever it was they were teaching him at Elland Road.

I had one of the old Leeds boys working with me at Portsmouth and then Tottenham, Joe Jordan. Genuinely tough, especially with the teeth out! I remember Joe as a fearsome player, but he was a great student of the game and a great coach. On one occasion, during a Spurs game against AC Milan, one of Joe's old clubs, it kicked off a bit, and their midfielder Gennaro Gattuso fancied himself and is over to our bench effing and blinding. Joe speaks good Italian, and so answered back, and it seemed to be getting a bit heated. What made me laugh is that Gattuso had married a Glaswegian and so there might have been some choice words in both languages being sprayed about. Joe kept in great nick and, had it gone too far, I reckon I know who my money would have been on. That's the difference between a genuine hard man and someone on the pitch who likes to play the big man.

I played with and against many genuine hard footballers. Tony Pulis at Bournemouth was tough and he would sort people out who might have had it coming. Roy Keane was one of the best midfielders I ever played against, he had everything, box-to-box, aggressive, goals, tempo, tackles,

but I would rather play against him than a few others. I mentioned previously that I'd rather face him than Patrick Vieira, purely because Patrick could be a bit trickier, a bit more spiteful. I'd rather face Roy than Dennis Wise too. Again, not on ability, but Dennis enjoyed leaving it on you. He certainly wasn't alone in that, but we'd meet up with England camps and he'd have a laugh about the stud marks he might have left with you the week before.

You could see Roy coming. It was never by stealth. Dennis would do it in a different way, sneak up where you didn't know he'd be. He was a great player with a cute baby face, but be fooled at your peril. Roy started out like that, an innocent-looking kid from Cork, but at Manchester United he did grow into this very intense midfielder. He had such an elite mindset, it was all about winning, driving people on. He was more fierce with his own players than opponents. Teammates would get it if standards dropped. I loved that about him. I always thought that I'd have loved to have played with Roy. Paul Ince would do that with me, when we played together, and I think I played my best football alongside him. It was very much a Manchester United thing. Probably a Sir Alex Ferguson thing too.

Roy did have a way of thinking about his next victim, though. We played Manchester United once. I was at Tottenham by then. I go in for a challenge and I catch Phil Neville late. Roy walks over to me. He wouldn't say much to me usually, but this time he says, 'Was that for your mate?'

I don't know what he means.

'What?'

'I said, is that for your mate?'

'What are you talking about?'

'McManaman.'

I had no idea what Macca had to do with it, or why Roy was bringing him up, but I found out that, the week before, Phil Neville had smashed Macca and so, by Roy's way of thinking, I must have been seeking some sort of revenge and retribution. No, Roy, it was just because, like everyone, I simply liked kicking Phil! I actually love Phil. And, by the way, he kicked me back more than a few times.

Steven Gerrard was a brilliantly tough young footballer when I was still at Liverpool, and you just knew he was going on to great things. Yes, there was the ability, the eye for a pass, the skill to ping it, but he was also, from the off, willing and able to get stuck in. Remember his early days, when he would launch himself into a tackle, especially in the Merseyside derbies, and by doing so slide into the hearts of Liverpool fans everywhere.

Today, the hard man is all but extinct, a relic of the game's past, and for many that is a good thing. Maybe the game, like some tackles, got too far over the top, but while bad tackles should be outlawed, it remains a contact sport and that must not change.

We all love a bit of skill in midfield, a cross-field pass to feet or a Cruyff turn, but a crunching, two-footed, sliding challenge that wins the ball and sends someone flying still has the power to bring the roof off even the most modern of English stadiums. The fans' favourite, in this country, is still the lad who gives his all, puts himself about and gets stuck in, week in and week out. It might be changing, our game might be on the brink of a more cerebral mindset, but while names like Billy Whitehurst remain in the memory, football will always be a hard man's sport.

Chapter 9

Earning a Bob or Two

HARRY

There was a time when my old man, an old docker from the East End of London, was one of Liverpool Football Club's most ardent supporters. Every other week, for every home game, my dad would get himself up to Liverpool – to cheer on the Reds, of course, but it was his grandson he was there to see. My dad took so much pleasure from watching Jamie play for one of the great clubs of European football, but despite those grand surroundings, his routine was always very basic.

He would get up early, and my mum would head to the local bakery to get some freshly baked crusty bread, and she would make him a cheese, mustard and pickle roll, with plenty of butter. But she would always make one extra, so that after the game Dad could pass it on to Jamie. He'd always loved those rolls, ever since he was a small boy. That wasn't going to change now he was in Liverpool's midfield.

After each game, Jamie would get dressed, come up and see Dad, have a chat about the game, usually celebrate a good win, and then Jamie, along with his teammate and great pal, Steve McManaman, would give Dad a lift back to Lime Street Station. In the car, Jamie would receive his cheese roll. After a while, though, there was a problem.

Dad called me one day, and he said, 'Harry, I feel terrible.'

'Why's that, Dad?'

'Well, each week I go up, and each week I get a lift back to the train station, and I give Jamie his roll, but I don't have one for Macca.'

It turns out that my mum was worried too, as she thought Steve McManaman needed fattening up a bit, so, from then on, Dad was going to the match with three cheese, mustard and pickle rolls, two of them for England international footballers.

The next time I was over at my parents' place, I said, 'Mum, Dad, they're both on about thirty thousand pounds a week, they can buy all the rolls they bloody well want.'

It didn't matter, the rolls kept coming.

Since then, the rolls have stopped, but the modern footballer now earns even more dough. As a manager, I witnessed the changes that came with the Premier League and the explosion in television money. Suddenly the whole world wanted to watch our game and, to stay ahead, the clubs needed the best players, and that meant paying them.

JAMIE

Money is a major part of the game, you can't get away from that, and it has been since I was a young player making my way at Liverpool. I don't want to sound like the old guard, and I certainly benefited from the riches on offer, but I do worry now that kids sometimes want to become footballers because of what they might earn.

I see some youngsters coming through and money is the first thing on their minds. When I was a kid, it was never about being a footballer for the money, because there was none. You made a decent living, but there were no riches, no footballers when I was growing up were set for life. It was just about making it, getting into a first team and the ultimate prize of being an international footballer. Maybe the biggest dream you had was getting on *A Question of Sport*.

My transfer to Liverpool got a lot of publicity. I'm sixteen and I'm the most expensive teenager in the game, and suddenly I am up in a new city and away from my parents, but the club looked after me. I was put in digs with two lovely families, so lovely that even when I was

a regular first-team player at the club and playing for England, I stayed with the Colliers – Alan and Janet and their kids, Mark and Joanne. A posh bachelor pad in town? No thanks. Give me a lovely family and a home-cooked meal.

For years, I had my Peugeot 309. I remember driving into the players' car park, and seeing Mike Marsh, our midfielder, get out of a nice Mercedes. Nothing major, but I did like it, and I remember thinking that one day I might be able to buy that off him.

In time, I was on £650 a week. Not bad at all, but I was playing well, and so myself and my pal, Don Hutchison, got a call to go and see Graeme Souness. It was quite a short conversation. 'You're both doing well, here's the new contract.'

We took a look. Both of us were being offered a grand a week. Good money, but then Graeme said sign it now. I was confused. We had to sign it now or the offer was gone? I wanted to talk to my dad. I didn't have an agent but my dad knew the game and I wanted his input. Don had no such hesitation.

'Where's the pen?' he said before signing it.

I shrugged and thanked Graeme, but I wasn't going to rush it. So I passed on it. The following year, I was playing even better, and when I got another offer, it was even better too. Don was fuming.

When the Premier League started in 1992, the money coming in was a slow burner but I do remember the news that our teammate, John Barnes, was getting £10,000 a week. It was big news, but to those of us playing with him, it didn't seem enough. The wages that players were getting were beginning to receive a lot of attention, and as those figures grew, the question seemed to be, did we deserve it?

It used to be all very quick. Two minutes at the most. A new season, into the manager's office.

'Hi Harry,' Ron would say. 'Come in, sit down.'

'Thanks, Mr Greenwood.'

'You've done well, we're pleased with you, there's another ten quid a week, and an extra fiver appearance money.'

There was no going away to mull over the offer.

'Thank you, Mr Greenwood,' and off you went home to tell the wife you'd got a £10 pay rise.

It just wasn't a concern. I'm sure the players around in 1961 were very grateful for Jimmy Hill's efforts and the abolition of the maximum wage that saw Johnny Haynes become the first £100-a-week player, but when I started playing and throughout the 1960s, money was never a big issue. We had Bobby Moore, the greatest, England's captain, a star, but even when he came back having lifted the World Cup, nothing changed. There was no demand for more cash, no ultimatums about leaving. Players just didn't leave clubs, unless the clubs wanted them to.

Player power? There was none.

Fame? We'd get a group of local lads at the gate wanting an autograph but that was it.

I stayed at my parents' house on the estate until I was twenty-one and got married. There was no such thing as celebrity in the game. Billy Wright, the England captain, had married one of the Beverley Sisters, a pop group in the 1950s, and that got some headlines, but otherwise, we were still just local lads playing for local teams, and the most we could hope for was a well-poured pint down the Blind Beggar or the Black Lion.

There was no feeling of fame. The game would end at Upton Park and by 5.30, we were in the Lion having a pint with our mates, all of them Hammers. We'd have a chat about the game but then minds turned to a Saturday night out. As I say, there were a few autograph hunters at Chadwell Heath, and we would always stop and sign them, but that was it. Mooro was obviously the guy most of them wanted to see, and he was great with them.

'Right, boys,' he'd say as he'd leave the training ground and would suddenly be surrounded by them all. 'Line up, line up against the wall, that's the only way.' They'd then all line up and one by one he'd sign their books.

I'd been turned down for a signature by a very rude old West Ham player when I was a kid and it affected me so, like all our lads, I'd be out there signing the books too.

That happened to me too! I was at a charity match with Dad. George Best among others was playing, and there were a few celebrities there too. I guess it was an early version of Soccer Aid. I was very young, collecting some autographs. I went up to one of the stars of the old sitcom, *Hi-de-Hi!* I'll never forget it. When I asked for his signature, he looked down at me, and he said, 'Go away.' I couldn't believe it, and he went on. 'What are you even doing here? This place is not for kids.'

Dad was furious. I'd never seen him like that. Luckily the actor left because Dad was on the warpath. 'I'll fuckin' knock him out,' Dad was saying. I think he would have too. Think of the headlines if that had happened.

It did stay with me, though, and it was probably a good thing to experience at a young age because I always tried to stop and sign for people, 99 per cent of the time. I might have been holding one of my boys at some point and physically couldn't, or there are the obvious ones where a guy is clearly a professional making money from you. They're the ones who bring a load of photos, and you know they are going on eBay the next day. But otherwise, stopping and taking some time to make a kid's day is no bother, is it? I do see footballers who drive on past kids, and I wonder why. Maybe they were never denied an autograph like me when they were young. It still upsets me. I never even liked *Hi-de-Hi!*

At Liverpool, there would always be a gang of kids outside the training ground at Melwood, and the likes of Macca and Robbie Fowler would always stop until everyone had been seen. By the mid- to late 1990s, both of those local guys and myself were playing well, playing for England, and after 1995, when the Bosman ruling came into play giving footballers more freedom of movement at the end of a contract, things changed further for players. At Liverpool, there had been some concern about Macca's contract and while eventually they would lose him to Real Madrid, they were quicker to offer myself and Robbie new deals.

I didn't want to leave, I loved the club, the fans were great, I got on with Roy Evans, and we had big hopes that we could win things. I had a couple of years still on my contract, I was playing well, working hard, and so the club called me in as they wanted to offer me a new deal. The great thing about Liverpool was that they wanted to look after their players. Some clubs try to play games, they look to hamstring the players financially, but I always found Liverpool fair. There were no games, just a confirmation and respect for the work I was putting in.

I remember going into a meeting about the contract. Roy was there along with David Moores, the chairman, who I loved, and the great Peter Robinson, a stalwart at the club as chief executive. They were sitting around this big table, and then on a speakerphone there was my dad. It was quite simple: the club had looked at what other midfielders were making, and come up with what they felt I was worth. The wage was great, and then I remember seeing the signing-on fee, and there were a lot of zeroes. As a young man, you do think, 'bloody hell'.

Dad was happy, proud of the hard work I had put in. I was ecstatic. It was a huge amount of money and I never took it for granted, but to be rewarded by the club was a special feeling. Robbie would have (deservedly) got more than that, and it was testimony to the way Sky's television money was moving into the game and how clubs were using it either to get the players they wanted or to keep the ones they had.

I may sound biased, but Sky changed everything. The Spanish and Italian leagues were always streets ahead of ours. The superstar footballers all went to clubs in those countries, but as the First Division morphed into the Premier League, that all (slowly) changed, and while, yes, that is hugely down to commercial revenue, there is no doubt that the exposure that Sky brought to everything lifted the whole game.

It wasn't an overnight thing. At first, there were bands on the pitch at half-time, there were dancing girls and it all seemed a bit American, a bit tacky maybe, but in time that razzmatazz was made real by the action on the pitch, not off it. As the money grew so did the quality

of footballer, and now it is the most watched league on the planet.

I remember Rodney Marsh, one of the original pundits on Sky, once saying that there would be a day soon when a footballer earned a hundred grand a week. Everyone laughed.

We were at West Ham when the Premier League launched. I had become Billy Bonds's assistant and we were in the old Second Division, which became the First Division (and is now the Championship). It all seemed a bit confusing, and we all thought it was merely a name change, and a stupid one at that. It took a while but then I started to see the changes. Great players were arriving, and then, being the manager at Upton Park, things like players' agents started to make contact.

It was a bit of a culture shock. Agents? I was left thinking about some players, 'Who do you think you are, having one?' and slowly but surely more and more of them were buzzing about. Suddenly phone calls from agents started to be a bigger part of a manager's routine than scouting. The days of going to games, watching a player and taking a gamble on him were disappearing. Now it was agents calling the shots, and soon clubs would turn to analysts and their data-driven information, until it became a case of managers often not even choosing their new players.

I do remember the first agent, or one of them anyway. He lived near us on the south coast and became a mate, a guy called Dennis Roach. Dennis was a shrewd operator. He had some massive overseas names, and he had been involved in the first £1 million transfer when Trevor Francis went from Birmingham to Nottingham Forest in 1979. He also looked after Johan Cruyff, and he had done the deal to get Mark Hughes over to Barcelona in 1986. Dennis did a lot of overseas deals, and there was almost a moment when he persuaded Jamie to go abroad.

I was about twenty-one years old. I was doing well at Liverpool, and with Dennis living near Dad and knowing him well, I got to talking to him, and with moves abroad a speciality of his, it shouldn't have surprised me that he had a proposal. AS Roma. I'm not sure if Dennis knew about my love of Italian football growing up, but he came to me and said Roma were interested, and if I was, we could make the move happen.

I won't lie, it sparked my imagination. This was Italian football in the early 1990s: Channel 4, Gazza, iconic. I also thought that Serie A might suit my game. My brother Mark was all over it. 'Let's go!' he was saying. He was coming with me. Full Jimmy Five-Bellies. He was buying a Vespa, the whole lot. To be fair, if I hadn't been at Liverpool I would have seriously considered it, and to this day I wonder what might have happened if I had;

to me and my brother. I couldn't leave, though. I loved the club too much, and my teammates, so that flirtation with the Italian game remained just that, a flirtation.

That was interesting. A move out to Italy might have suited Jamie, the style of play there definitely would have, but I understood his reasons for staying. I also understood that the game was changing, players in the Premier League were more and more under the microscope. The front-page journalists were just as interested in them as the football writers. Who were they seeing, where were they going out, how much were they earning, what were they spending it on? Maybe there was a thought that if he moved abroad he might get away from all that. Liverpool were a hard club to leave, though, and I understood Jamie dismissing the idea.

That attention didn't cease, though. Footballers were all over the papers, the magazines, on the television. The Dentist's Chair incident out in Hong Kong in 1996 definitely brightened that spotlight, and then along came players like David Beckham, megastars. Like Billy Wright in my day, an England captain, marrying a pop star. Maybe the generations weren't that different after all?

We got it in the neck at Liverpool, when we were nicknamed 'The Spice Boys'. A group of young lads, always out, not taking life or football very seriously. It was a

preconception, and one that didn't bother us. We knew how hard we were working, and we knew the task we had – trying to beat Alex Ferguson's Manchester United – could only be achieved through that hard work.

The thing that did us, though, was the 1996 FA Cup final. It was an opportunity to beat United. We had given them a great game at Old Trafford that season and beaten them at our place, and going to Wembley we really felt we had a chance. We played badly, but so did they; they won through a silly goal we gave away. But what people battered us with was the white suits we wore prior to the game.

There are two things about those damn suits. First of all, if we'd just played well and won, then we'd all probably still have them in our closets, and we'd be laughing about how bad they looked. I'd love to be laughing about them, trying on for old times' sake, but we lost, and they will always be the reason why. However wrong that actually is.

The second thing is, why the hell didn't someone just say no? I was a young footballer, but I still think I had a strong enough character to object. There were plenty of us in that squad who might have said no. We had the club suits at the ready, but instead there we were, looking like ice-cream salesmen, and the images will haunt us all forever. I am not having Alex Ferguson's remarks, though, that United saw us in them and immediately knew they'd win. That's nonsense. They played just as badly as us.

I had a great young generation at West Ham in the mid- to late 1990s – Frank Lampard, Rio Ferdinand, Joe Cole and Michael Carrick – and we were mindful of looking after them. We knew that new type of fame was going to come around, and we tried to do as much as we could to protect them. There is, though, only so much you can do.

We were lucky. All those guys were grounded. Frank's dad would be all over him if he stepped out of line, Rio came from a good family, Joe Cole was not the type to go out, and Michael Carrick was all about the football. If a player came into training and he had a flash new car, you'd try to take him down a peg or two, ask him why he needs to drive something like that. But, at the end of the day, it was their money and you could only guide them and help them focus on their football.

It wasn't like it was all new. My generation had George Best, the first real footballing superstar. Players had always tried to make a bit of extra cash. George had his boutiques, Alan Ball signed a deal and wore white football boots . . . it's always been there, and you can't begrudge the players getting well paid. The game has to take care, though. It's big business, yes, and the players give big entertainment, but being of the old school, I do worry about the future.

Some clubs try to do what they can. Liverpool don't allow the younger players to have any car with anything bigger than a 1.3 engine. That might make people laugh

but when these kids, yet to play for the first team, can be earning twenty or thirty grand a week, that can be very unhealthy and we have to make sure that there are guidelines in place to help them.

I do worry that some kids want to play football just to achieve a level of fame. What we need is characters who love the game. Dad's generation was full of them, and when I was playing, there were all sorts of players who refused to blend in. That's why I like Jack Grealish and Cole Palmer, not just because they try to do things in the game that are off-the-cuff, but because they dare to be different.

Money is no longer an issue for so many footballers. The watches, the clothes, the cars, the houses, they are set, but I just hope that the love of football, the buzz they got when they started out, working hard to make it, never leaves them. I also hope that they continue to enjoy their nan's cheese, mustard and pickle rolls, with extra butter.

Chapter 10

The Greatest Teams

JAMIE

Bournemouth were my team, really. I was more interested in playing but, as a boy, it was at Dean Court that I would watch and cheer and support a team. There was no glory, no open-top buses, no big European nights, but I knew every bit of the place. I could help out in the dressing rooms, I could chat to the groundsman, John, and I could sit in the same seat every other week, supporting the lads who I had watched train all week, and hope that my dad would come away with the three points that would mean the world to him and the few thousand who had come to watch.

That was my footballing world. I had those posters up all over my bedroom walls of the individual superstars playing in our game and abroad, but when it came to teams, other than the odd visit to Luton to watch their lot, it was all about Bournemouth.

One night, at home, *Sportsnight* came on the television, and suddenly there was a team on, a team we all knew were doing well that season, but there they were and that year's Goal of the Season competition was dedicated completely to them. It was 1988, Liverpool would gallop to the title with a brand of football that took the breath away, and to commemorate just how good the team was, ten of their goals were on show for the public to choose the best.

That immediately got my attention. Ten superb goals. A few from John Aldridge (his volley against Nottingham Forest won), a few from Peter Beardsley, and the other four from Ray Houghton, Steve McMahon, Steve Nicol and John Barnes. A team had never seemed to dominate like that in the past, not even Liverpool's former incarnations, and when you look back at how they went about it, the fluid, skilful football that they played, it is little wonder that there are many at the club today who believe that was their very best.

I had grown up knowing that Liverpool had great teams, teams with a style that didn't seem to change. Good defenders, comfortable ball players all over the pitch, and then Kenny Dalglish able to feed Ian Rush, goals, and the game won. This team was more extravagant. Sure, they still had Alan Hansen dictating things from the back, but Kenny had built a new way. Beardsley replaced him, all skill and high energy, John Aldridge replaced Ian Rush, the same eye for goal but more suited to width, and John Barnes, well he brought the width, but he also brought joy to the punters and misery to defenders.

Along with that trio, you had McMahon, Ronnie Whelan, Nicol, Gary Gillespie and Houghton, who was an extremely intelligent footballer. We all talk today about the press and playing with intensity as some sort of modern fad, but watch some of that team's games. John Aldridge's effort against Arsenal, when Steve McMahon, instead of letting the ball run out for a throw-in, keeps the ball on with the sole of his boot, bounces back into play off the advertising boards, drives forward and Aldridge gets his goal. I would watch them on *Match of the Day* and wonder, what would it be like to play in that team. A few years later, most of them were still there when I signed for the club.

I also wonder about what that team might have achieved in Europe. The five-year European ban given to English clubs following the Heysel stadium disaster in 1985 put paid to that, but isn't it a fascinating thought to think about how Kenny's team would have got on against Arrigo Sacchi's AC Milan in the following year's European Cup? What a mouthwatering final that would have been.

Paolo Maldini at left-back and Roberto Donadoni dealing with Houghton and Nicol on Liverpool's right, or would it be the other way around? McMahon and Whelan competing with Frank Rijkaard and Carlo Ancelotti in midfield, John Barnes getting the better of Mauro Tassotti, John Aldridge trying to stretch Franco Baresi. Individually, the Italians look the better side, but you have to remember what a great unit that Liverpool team were.

The big match-up would be between Alan Hansen and Marco van Basten and Ruud Gullit. I am good friends with Ruud and when he talks about van Basten, his face lights up, but if there was a defender around at the time who might have coped, it was Alan. You might have Milan as slight favourites, but if Barnes and Beardsley were on their game, a wily Kenny Dalglish might have left with that wonderful smile on his face.

HARRY

There were Bill Shankly's Liverpool teams that I played against, and then there were Bob Paisley's and Joe Fagan's that I watched, but they all boiled down to the same thing, the same thing all great teams have, and it's great players. That sounds simple, but it's true. Ron Greenwood would say, stick eleven good players on a pitch together, and even if none of them speak the same language the team will do well.

Bob and then Joe had their teams very much speaking the same language, and it was all done very simply. Great scouting, spotting great players, training them, trusting them and letting them get on with things. Graeme Souness always makes me laugh when he tells me about getting a bit nervous before his debut, and going to Joe and saying he still didn't know how they wanted him to play. Joe told him to 'fuck off' and said, 'We've spent all this money on you and you're asking us how to play football.' Graeme never asked any questions again.

I was at Fulham once to watch a game. They were playing Joe Fagan's Liverpool in the League Cup, and he was sat in front of us in the directors' box. Shortly into the game, a guy shouted down to him – they were old army buddies, and Joe invited him to sit next to him. I was close by and I can tell you, Joe didn't watch a minute of the game. They were chatting away about old times, their wives, the good old days in the army. At half-time, Joe got up and said see you later. I was left sitting there thinking, how the hell is he going to give a teamtalk about a game he hasn't watched? It dawned on me that that wasn't how he and his Liverpool team had to work.

The team I loved to watch, in the 1960s, was Jock Stein's Celtic side that won everything, including the European Cup in 1967. What a side they were. Quick, front-foot football, and we all loved that they were a team consisting of players only within throwing distance of Celtic Park.

As a winger, I loved Jimmy Johnstone. Jinky was such a clever wide man, a bag of tricks with end product. Scotland had a habit of producing them. Players like Willie Henderson at Rangers. Wingers who would dribble all day, but Jinky was the best and the Lisbon Lions, as that European Cup-winning side became known, were the team to see.

Prior to Celtic, there were the teams we couldn't see but we were told about. The Hungarians of 1953 who taught England a lesson about where the game was heading, and Real Madrid who won the first five European Cups after the competition started in 1955. I had been lucky enough to see Matt Busby's Babes at Highbury, and what a youthful joy they were, but when I started playing, and training with them as a boy, Tottenham were the best in England.

The 1960–1 double-winning team of Dave Mackay, Bobby Smith, John White and Danny Blanchflower, managed by Bill Nicholson. I saw them up close, but it was Danny who most caught the eye. He was very much the brains of the outfit. He once told me that he had gone with Northern Ireland to play Brazil. They had a player, before Garrincha even, who could bend the ball from free-kicks, and it was Danny who devised the plan to build a wall to make life harder for him. His teammates must have thought he was mad, but soon they and the whole world were doing it. With that level of intelligence, it's little surprise Tottenham were so successful.

In the modern era, there is no more successful club than Manchester United, and if we are talking about great teams, when it comes to Alex Ferguson's tenure, there are three to choose from. The first was his 1994 double-winning team. Ferocious in pace and strength. Ryan Giggs, Lee Sharpe or Andrei Kanchelskis on the wings, Eric Cantona, the icing on the cake, and stalwarts like Steve Bruce and Denis Irwin in defence. Down the middle was Mark Hughes. I grew up loving Sparky. That volley he scored, a scissor kick, against Spain for Wales was my favourite ever goal. He was so hard to play against, facing goal, or with his back to it, and he wasn't afraid of leaving a bit on you. Hard as nails.

The team in 1999, that was special too. The Class of '92, all grown up. David Beckham, Gary and Phil Neville, Giggs still doing it, Jaap Stam dominating at the back, Peter Schmeichel still in goal barking orders. They won the treble, including the Champions League, but we might have stopped them. Liverpool were one up at Old Trafford early on in the FA Cup run. I made a challenge high up the pitch. Graham Poll blew up for a foul, but – and not that I am bitter after quarter of a century – it was never a foul. Had he let me play on, two of us were in, and I reckon it's 2–0. Instead we let them back in and they won 2–1. As I say, I am not bitter. I promise.

They were some side. So was the 2008 Champions League-winning team, with a forward line of Cristiano

Ronaldo, Carlos Tevez and Wayne Rooney. You can't get much better than that strike force. If you ask me to pick, out of the three sides, who I rate most, I'll find it hard, but I can't see past the 1999 treble team, specifically because I can't see past a midfield of Roy Keane and Paul Scholes. That's what swings it in that team's favour.

What all three sides had, though, was bravery, and that came from the manager. Fergie was a manager who had no problem with throwing on attackers, not gung-ho or for the sake of it right at the end, but whenever the team needed it, even if the risk of losing was high. Ferguson's United teams also, when winning, would never take their foot off the gas, and their fans never left a game thinking they'd been short changed.

One manager who took on and rattled Ferguson's sides was José Mourinho. When he arrived at Chelsea in 2004 and built a team that won back-to-back titles, some felt the team wasn't as pleasing on the eye as previous title winners. That might have sounded strange because they had Frank in midfield, Arjen Robben, Joe Cole, Didier Drogba and Damien Duff, and much of their play was all power and guile. I think where some people were less romantic about them was because, at 2–0 up, they would often put on the handbrake. Holding midfielders might replace the more creative players, as if to say that's enough for the day. Thank you and goodbye.

However José Mourinho's sides were regarded, they were unrelenting and shook the game, and they shook Ferguson. Not many had. Kenny's Blackburn did it for one season in 1995. A great side led by the brilliant Alan Shearer, a hybrid of Wayne Rooney and Harry Kane. He was some player, a goal machine. Blackburn couldn't maintain their success, though, and instead that task of being a constant thorn in Ferguson's side fell to Arsène Wenger, and his two great teams are right up there in the conversation anyone has about the very best in the Premier League era.

The first team that Wenger took to glory, in 1998, was powerful, very hard to get the better of, and with the old back four to shore it all up. For me, though, the greatest team, the best I ever played against anyway, was the 2004 Invincibles. I had moved to Tottenham by the time they were doing their thing, and the games against them were as hard as I had anywhere.

There was so much power in that side. Sol Campbell at the back, one of the great English defenders, alongside him at left-back was Ashley Cole. The greatest English left-back of all-time? I think so. Patrick Vieira, Ray Parlour, Gilberto Silva, made up an all-action midfield and then you had Robert Pires and Dennis Bergkamp causing havoc, but still big athletes. The whole thing was sprinkled with the magic dust of Thierry Henry. The football he played was from another planet.

We played them at White Hart Lane in the April of 2004. Arsenal needed just a draw to take the title, and we ran out to face them with a threadbare team, and in the first half, they absolutely chinned us. We were chasing shadows. I was in midfield with Michael Brown, and Vieira and Silva, for all our endeavour, ran us ragged. I came in at half-time, we were 2–0 down, and I was shattered. We all were.

Paul Robinson, the keeper, came in and lost his temper. He started screaming that we needed to get closer, to start making tackles. I liked Paul, but I wasn't having that. 'What do you fucking think we're trying to do?' I shouted back at him. I had been doing doggies all half, and I wasn't letting a goalkeeper tell me to work harder. Robbie Keane was equally as incensed, and he let Paul have it, too. I think Paul pulled a masterstroke of man-management, though, because somehow we went out there, I scored one, and then Robbie got a late equaliser. It was an unexpected moral victory, but Arsenal were able to celebrate after as champions and they would go on to be unbeaten in the league that season. As I say, they were the best I ever shared a pitch with.

Arsène Wenger's early teams at Highbury were fantastic. All power and flair. They reminded me a lot of Don Revie's Leeds United teams in the 1960s and particularly the early 1970s. Not everyone liked Leeds and even those who admired them found it hard to love them. I was a fan. I had never seen such a well-balanced side. Two great centre-halves in Norman Hunter and Jackie Charlton. The full-backs were exceptional: Terry Cooper and Paul Reaney. Up and down, all action. Peter Lorimer, Johnny Giles, Billy Bremner; not many could live with them when it came to skill or grit. Up front, Allan Clarke and Mick Jones, two six-foot centre-forwards who could also mix it. Great with their feet and their heads. It was a phenomenal side, one of our best.

There might have been better football teams, on paper, but has there been an English club side that gave the game a bigger fairy tale than Leicester in 2016? I can still be walking or driving or doing something mundane, and the thought pops back into my head. 'How the fuck did that happen?'

It's a question that might come to me for the rest of my days, and it may never be matched in terms of achievement. Take a close look, though, and it is like Dad says; it's all about good coaching, great recruitment and a group of very good footballers. Yes, there might have been some magic, some unexplained alchemy, but in the end it was those magic ingredients that gave the Premier League exactly what it needed; a reminder that money and power aren't everything.

Being a pundit, working on the games that season, we all might have thought, look at Leicester winning the odd game, isn't that nice? Don't forget, they had almost gone down the previous season and this run of form came from absolutely nowhere. They lost to Liverpool and Arsenal, and people wondered if that was that. Champions League qualification became the pipe dream, but then they found another gear. They went to Manchester City, and won 3–1 in February, and didn't look back.

On and on they went. Kasper Schmeichel, Robert Huth, Danny Drinkwater, Danny Simpson, Wes Morgan; names that alone might not inspire visions of trophy-ladened glory, but together, at the top of their game and with Riyad Mahrez and Jamie Vardy unleashing their quality on all-comers, teams didn't know what had hit them.

When they received the trophy, I was at the King Power. Suddenly Andrea Bocelli is up on stage belting out opera, and the whole thing felt like a surreal but wonderful dream. I got chatting with the late Craig Shakespeare, one of the coaches at the club, and asked him about how they played. I was especially interested in the midfield.

He told me they had a system. On the right of the midfield they have N'Golo Kanté, in the middle is Danny Drinkwater, and on the left of the midfield they have N'Golo Kanté. It summed it up brilliantly. Kanté was just unreal that season. Some call him a holding midfielder. A Claude Makélélé type. Do me a favour?

He was everywhere and within that great team and that great story, he is up there with the great individual performances any season has ever seen.

There was talk that Hollywood might make a movie about Leicester City's Premier League victory, and as box office as it was, the most glorious team of them all, the one that would have me rushing to any cinema anywhere, was the Brazil team that won the 1970 World Cup.

What a summer of football that was, and what a side Brazil were. None of us had seen anything like them before. The games started, we all watched England actually give them a great game in the group stages, losing narrowly by one goal, but as it went on, we'd all rush to our, now colour, televisions, to make sure we saw their next game.

I had actually bought a colour TV, from a guy in a café in east London. This was the first World Cup shown in colour, and so when this guy came in and told me and Roger Cross, my teammate at West Ham, that he had a couple of high-tech new colour sets and they were ours for a oner each, we stupidly jumped at the chance. We both agreed and this guy drove one to my house, not letting me help him carry it, and then on to Roger's. He then took our money, only for us to find out that both sets were empty shells. We'd bought two £100 drink cabinets.

Still, it didn't deter us from getting our hands on legit televisions later, and enjoying Brazil in full technicolour.

And that's what they were. In their bright yellow shirts, it was like watching football from another world, and when they dissected a very good Italian team in the final, beating them 4–1, the stuff played by Jairzinho, Carlos Alberto, Rivellino, Tostão and Pelé had us all purring. I have seen many great sides since, I have seen them close up, played against some of them, but I have never seen a better team than Brazil during that glorious summer of 1970.

I grew up with stories about that side, looking for old VHS tapes of the team, and now I can scroll through YouTube (if you haven't, you should), drooling at the goals, the almost goals and the audacity of some of their play, from defence to attack.

As a boy, and even a young man, that team seemed mystical, unreachable, like a moment in history that would never be repeated. But, then I went to see Pep Guardiola's Barcelona side and everything I had seen on old video tapes and on my laptop was there in real time, in front of me. Dad might disagree, and he might be right that even Pep's team play second fiddle to 1970 Brazil, but for me the greatest team I've seen live is the Barcelona team that took Manchester United apart in the 2011 Champions League final.

I was lucky enough to cover Champions League football for Sky for a bit, and to move around the great cities of Europe, enjoying a glass of wine and a nice plate

of tapas, before watching Messi, Xavi and Iniesta do their thing; well, I used to go back to my hotel after and wonder what I had done to be given the greatest job in the world.

I actually loved the earlier incarnation of the team with Yaya Touré in the Sergio Busquets position, but to see them take England's best team apart at Wembley that night was to see football change in front of my very eyes.

That's why it was so jaw dropping when Pep Guardiola came to England, and with him came that style of football that today everyone from the upper reaches of the Premier League to the Dog and Duck over the park on a Sunday morning tries to recreate. Some don't like Manchester City's style of play under Pep, saying it is too possession based, but that's how I have always liked my football. Protecting the ball, finding the right pass, but never for the sake of it..

It's why, in my opinion, Pep is the greatest manager of the Premier League era. Many will disagree and, of course, Alex Ferguson's level of success is frighteningly good, but Fergie, for all the trophies, never changed the game, his was about building teams and I so respect that, but Pep did that, won everything, and made a huge difference to how people play and view football. It's an argument for the pub, and while it can't be won, I am sure of just how special it has been to watch Guardiola's sides play.

I reckon we'd have given them a game at Dean Court though . . .

Chapter 11
My Dad

JAMIE

It only takes a matter of seconds. That's all. On the many occasions my dad has joined me for one of my sons' many games of football, we will be standing on a park, or sat in a stand, and within seconds he'll say it. 'That kid can play.' It's a simple declaration, his eyes have run over the kids playing or starting to play and, without fail, those words will come out of his mouth.

He's never wrong. It's a gift. I don't tend to question his eyes or his logic. I never say a word now about individuals but I sit and I wait, knowing that a pearl of wisdom is about to drop. He never lets me down. 'That kid can play.'

For so long, ever since I was a young boy myself and he was watching my early forays into the game, he has been able to stand quietly, watch a group of players, cast those seemingly magic eyes over them, and quickly point out where the talent lies.

Dad is one of those guys: a very real football man. He lives and breathes the game. A park match cannot be passed without his glare falling on it like he was scouting a World Cup final. It's just in his bones. Like kids learning to walk, talk, read and write, Dad's love of football was ingrained in him from the earliest age. An only child, Dad simply followed and hero-worshipped his own dad, Harry Snr, whose love for the game before and after the war could only be described as obsessive.

It's a modern family trait. I certainly have it, and some of my sons, even the very youngest, show real signs of having it, and when it came to my dad and my grandad, a feel for the mechanics of a football match and the players who play it was always natural.

From taking my young dad to games all over London and beyond, my pops – despite the frustration that the war had curtailed his own (very real) dreams of playing league football – was a constant companion in Dad's and my careers. Throughout Dad's playing days, and certainly through mine, while he was alive, he was an ever-present. Pops would have watched any game. The sight of floodlights switching on anywhere was greeted with childlike pleasure, as if a Christmas tree had been turned on for the first time.

And it wasn't just that football enthusiasm that Pops brought to our lives. Like Dad, he could spot a player, knew all anyone could know about the game in and around the East End of London, and much of that knowledge would find its way into Dad's ear.

Managing West Ham, Dad had got a tip-off about a kid in Peckham, south London, but Millwall were interested. The fourteen-year-old was Rio Ferdinand and with the Lions being his local club, it was hard to tell with whom he might choose to play his football.

They knew he was good, but he was still a schoolboy, not yet signed on a professional contract, but one night with the West Ham youth team winning the prestigious South-East Counties Cup final, at Chelsea, a call from Pops to Dad probably fast-tracked a remarkable career. 'I've seen a kid playing for your lot tonight,' Pops said. 'In midfield. He's absolute mustard.'

I think Dad presumed he meant my cousin, Frank, but when Pops said his name was Ferdinand, Dad was confused.

'You must be mistaken, Dad,' he said. 'Young Rio is too young, he wouldn't have played tonight.'

'He did, and he was the best player on the pitch.'

With such glowing reports from an eye he always trusted, Dad knew that losing this talent to another local club would not do, and efforts were stepped up to turn on the charm, and to make sure it was at West Ham that the young man chose to sign. I remember being over at my parents', and sitting with Pops. I had broken into the Liverpool side, was close to my first England call-up, and Pops told me, 'Jamie, this kid close to signing for your dad: if he doesn't make it, we might as well all go home.'

Rio signed, and was fast-tracked out on loan to Bournemouth. While catching the eye on the south coast, Dad took a call. It was from Martin Edwards, the chairman at Manchester United. 'This kid, Rio Ferdinand, he's quite a player, isn't he?'

Dad agreed, and went on to tell the man with his hands on British football's loosest purse strings that his young asset was not for sale. Not for any money. 'One day, he'll be the best defender in Europe.'

Less than a decade later, Manchester United spent over thirty million quid on him. A world record for a defender. As ever, Dad wasn't wrong.

My very younger days playing football (always playing football) were greeted with less grandiose predictions than those that met a teenage Rio Ferdinand. Not because Dad thought I wasn't good enough to make it, it was just that he was very calm, and very unwilling to force a career on me from a young age.

When I was playing, for school teams or my local kids' teams, Dad would be there, but he would stand away from the other parents, and the game would always be taken in, but in silence. He never said a word. During the game, there was no distant voice from Dad, no manic words of advice, and even on the way home the feedback would be minimal. I think it helped that I was a trier, and my attitude was always OK.

You can't play brilliantly every game, and I think if I had sloped onto the field, not fancying it, moaning about the weather or not getting the ball, I think then there might have been something to say. If the tricks don't come off, if the passing or shooting are off, well that happens, but I think Dad was calmly assured that I was always putting my shift in, that I was getting stuck in, helping my teammates. That's what made him quietly happy.

I remember one game, it was an under-15 match at Bournemouth's ground, and I came off with a bit of a teenage mood on. I had been up against another kid in midfield, a kid who was very good, people knew about him, clubs were interested and that day he more than got the better of me. I had a bit of a sulk on, but on the way home, my dad calmly said, 'Well, you've seen the standard now, that's what you have to work towards, and that's what you have to be better than if you want to get to where you want to get to.'

The following year, the kid and I played against each other again, and I was on a mission to get on top of him. I had a good game, we won, and while Dad would have greeted me with nothing more than a smile after the match, it was little, subtle things like those words that guided me. Nothing mouthy, nothing vitriolic, and certainly no chest thumping.

Maybe it's weird, but we never had cross words. My mum too. You could count the small disagreements I've had with my parents on half a hand, and even when my dad was my manager, things were said calmly and without big emotion. He certainly never pushed me into a football career; there was only that still knowledge that I both loved the game and had a bit of talent. Shouting at us boys, even when we became teenagers, it just didn't happen.

Don't get me wrong, he has a side to him, and it's one I've seen close up, especially in my early days playing for him at Bournemouth. When Dad flipped, it was wise to duck. Or you might be wearing some pickle and mustard. As I've said, a dressing room's plate of rolls were the ideal thing to vent his anger on, and I've seen many cheese and ham sandwiches given wings over the years.

It was that side of Dad's character, that fire in his belly clearly only stoked by his passion for football, that actually convinced me when I was young that he'd never become a manager. Not because he lacked knowledge or ability – no one in my mind has ever known more about the game – but I heard from so many people that he wasn't cut out for it. That this fiery side to his footballing personality would hold him back.

'He's too mad, is Harry,' people would say, or, 'Your dad was always getting in trouble, there's no way he could hack it as a boss.' I presumed everyone was right because while I never saw him lose his temper at home with us boys, or be volatile when it came to what we might do with our lives, there were enough stories flying around about him losing his cool to suggest he would have to choose something else to keep him busy once he packed in playing.

Take how he left West Ham, as a player. Dad adored Ron Greenwood, his manager there, but after seven years playing for him, things took a turn. It was 1970, a few years before my arrival, and Dad, despite feeling he was playing well, was subbed off during a poor team performance at Upton Park.

Dad was feeling unloved by Ron, took the decision badly and walked slowly, very slowly from the field. Later, in the dressing room, Ron lost his rag with him (a rarity in itself), telling him in no uncertain terms that, next time, he runs off and he shows some respect.

Dad answered back, disagreeing with the decision, bemoaning the fact that it's always him getting subbed despite playing well, and a few other choice phrases a manager like Ron probably wasn't used to hearing. Ron stormed out of the room, and now fully revved up Dad picked up a bottle of lager from a post-match beer crate and threw it at the door, smashing it and emptying its suds all over the floor. Jimmy Greaves is said to have looked at the mess, looked at Dad and said, 'That's nice, you could have thrown an empty one.'

There were more stories, more tales of slight indiscipline from his playing days. That's why I think Dad was always on at me to be tidy, always reiterating the importance of time-keeping, being a good pro, keeping boots cleaned, being organised when I had a trial. Dad's time-keeping isn't great – he once missed a train taking him to England schoolboy trials – and I think he was adamant that the things that ever so slightly held his career back would not do the same to me.

People don't quite realise that when Dad was coming through at West Ham, he was considered one of if not the best young player in the country, and it was probably those little details in personality that might have stopped him reaching his full potential. That's probably what my dad would think, and so, with me trying to make it in the game, he took steps to make sure my potential was realised.

Dad wanted to manage, though, he persevered, and being such an innate football person, he was able to get non-league roles, and then the assistant manager's position at Bournemouth, before landing the main job there in 1983. There would be fallouts, life on a shoestring budget for any manager is tough, but Dad had his great mate Brian Tiler as his managing director, who, while not shy in giving it back to Dad at times, would keep him in check, could keep him calm, and so progress was made.

It was a tricky start, though. He was only the caretaker manager there when in 1982, for his first game, they went to Lincoln City and got absolutely annihilated. Even today he'll tell you the game should never have gone ahead due to a frozen pitch but, nevertheless, it did and they got beat by nine goals. I remember him coming home, and our mum telling us boys to keep quiet, so us boys stuck on our VHS version of *E.T.* that Dad had found from somewhere and kept well out of his way.

You knew to do that if the team lost. That never changed throughout his career. Everyone rightly knows him as Happy Harry, a great character, chirpy, but if the team lost, don't bother. I think a lot of managers have that, and Dad, with that managerial competitive streak . . . well, I knew as a boy not to approach. My brother Mark wasn't so clued up, and sometimes put his foot in it, and words might be had, but that's football management. Saturday night. A win and the family have a Chinese takeaway. Lose and it's silence until bedtime.

How lucky was Dad though? A nine-goal spanking on his first game as caretaker manager and he still gets the job. You have to be fortunate as a football manager, fortunate, charming and stubborn, and Dad can be all three. And so with a few better results he got the job, and thank goodness for that.

He wasn't a career man, though. He didn't have a plan. Dad doesn't do plans. He's not that type. If, after that disastrous start, Bournemouth would have turned him away, it is hard to say where the Redknapps would have ended up. It's hard to know if he would have got another go at management, had the career he had or even gone on to win *I'm a Celebrity . . . Get Me Out of Here!*

Dad loved football, wanted to work in it, but it's a results business and but for some perseverance on his and the club's part, his career might never have got off the ground. If he'd had to choose another path, he would have done OK, in anything. Dad's very streetwise and he tends to find a way, he's a survivor, but fortunately for him, for us and for several football clubs, he stuck in there and his life became all about football management.

And at Bournemouth, that life was a very happy one. As a teenager looking on, I could sense how much he loved it, how he enjoyed working, being around footballers, getting new ones in, building teams, good footballing teams. He was very content on the south coast and, as I say, there was no big plan, not that I knew of anyway, and so instead he carried on doing his thing down there.

I would go to places with him, my obsession for the game was taking control, Dad knew that, and so, at his side, I would attend meetings, be in dressing rooms, listen to discussions with Brian about players, about tactics, about footballers. The game was everything.

Dad had a bible. *Rothmans Football Yearbook*. That big blue book with all the stats and all the figures, that came out every summer. I never saw my dad read a book but I saw him plough through that book every year, his copy, like me, never far from his side, dog-eared and well-thumbed, on hand to give him any information he needed. The thing is, soon he didn't need to look through it. He had it memorised.

We'd be in the car, off to a match. Driving, he'd often talk about the team. 'I need a left-back,' or 'My right-wing needs reinforcing.' He loved assembling teams, and then he'd say, 'Go on, Jamie, test me.' So, I'd open the big blue *Rothmans*, and he'd say, 'Name a player, any player.' It was like a magician starting a card trick.

I'd be keen to catch him out, look for some obscure player, not realising there was no such thing as an obscure player. Not with Dad around. I'd give him a name.

'Right, left-sided midfielder, 373 games, Scunthorpe United and Halifax Town, 32 goals, born on 17 July 1959.'

He was the master. I never caught him out. Never mind *I'm a Celebrity*, Dad could have gone on *Mastermind*, and won, with his specialised subject, 'Lower League Footballers in the 1980s'.

When it came to making decisions about my own career, I'm not sure it was seeing Dad so happy at Bournemouth that made me choose to play for him, but I could see what a great coach he was, what a great footballing man he had become and how, with him, there was an easier path to what I wanted, first-team football.

Choosing Bournemouth over Tottenham, like I did, felt right. It felt like a clearer way in. I had trained with Spurs, really liked John Moncur Snr, the head of youth development there, and I enjoyed playing for them, but when that offer came in for me, it was no.

Most would have jumped at it, the money (while nothing big) was like nothing I had earned before or what Bournemouth could pay me, but I just didn't see any sight of the first team. That might sound arrogant or brave or both, but I wanted to learn, and I honestly felt that it was with my dad, one of the best coaches in the lower leagues, with whom I could do that.

I had played as a trainee at Spurs with a kid called Shaun Murray, a Geordie, signed from Newcastle and a lovely footballer. Big things were being said about him, but Shaun seemed to get lost in the system, and looking in, I noticed it and wanted to make sure that was not going to happen to me.

Dad quietly disagreed, of course, but he also respected my decision, and as ever was not going to dictate to me how to live my life and forge my path. So, Dad was now also my boss. As ever, things were pretty simple. I got in the team, I did all right, worked hard and got on with things.

I think it helped that Kenny came in for me quite quickly after that. I still waited, still played with Bournemouth, and Dad was great with me, not giving me preferential treatment, and the pros at the club, many of them seasoned, saw that I wasn't there because I was the boss's son, but that I worked hard, could play a little bit, and they treated me like they would any young player.

It was a great set of lads there, and importantly they were good football people. Tony Pulis had come in, Sean O'Driscoll, Kevin Bond, players who went on to have good managerial careers, and who already got the game. Dad got them and they got Dad, and so him bringing in his son was never going to ruffle feathers.

The thing is, and this goes for my whole career, Dad was never overbearing towards me and certainly not flash when it came to my progress. He wouldn't go on at people; even when I left for Liverpool, there was no boasting on his part and, in fact, he seemed a little bit embarrassed whenever he was asked about me. He was proud, sure, but he just wanted to quietly let me get on with things. That's how it had always been.

Don't get me wrong, if Dad lost it, those sandwiches would fly by my ears as ferociously as anyone else's, but on the whole things were smooth. On one occasion, though, he did embarrass me. We were playing at Grimsby. First of all, I'm sixteen and I had heard great things about the fish and chips up there. All the boys were going on about them, and as ever with away bus trips, it was decided that we would get a big order for the way home. The order was put in, and we get on with the game.

Excuse the pun but Grimsby battered us that day, 5–1. We were woeful, and we trudged back into the dressing room with not much to say for ourselves. The opposite goes for Dad. He's fuming, and with plenty to say. He's screaming his head off. Effing and blinding, and telling everyone just what he thinks of their performance.

I'd got on as a sub at 4–0, so the sandwiches flying around the room aren't aimed at me. My only thought is, who needs sandwiches when we have those fish and chips later? But Dad then stops, turns, points to me and says, 'If only you lot cared half as much as him, we'd have been all right.' It's the worst thing he could have said about me, and I wanted the floor to swallow me up. To be fair, the lads were great and saw the funny side of it, but when Dad then said, 'And if any of you clowns think you're having fish and chips tonight, you have got another think coming,' well, that was a double blow, and I probably gave him the cold shoulder for the rest of the night. I still haven't had fish from Grimsby.

Looking back, I wonder if Dad quietly wanted more than just fish and chips for his career. He certainly wasn't greedily seeking out Michelin stars but with his Bournemouth teams always having a reputation for good football, some might have wondered why, after nearly ten years at the club, something bigger hadn't come along?

Frankly, I don't think Dad cared. I sensed that achievements such as the 1987 promotion to the old Second Division (the league's then second tier) gave Dad the satisfaction he desired from the game and his work, and it is only looking back now that I wonder why no bigger jobs became available to this clearly talented young manager.

I think it came down to preconceptions, assumptions that actually stayed with Dad throughout his managerial career. The sense that he was the cheeky-chappy manager, that phrase 'wheeler-dealer' never far from people's lips when describing his work. The idea was that he was a great man-manager maybe, but with the game apparently getting more and more technical, it was deemed by some that it didn't suit his talents.

That annoys me so much. First of all, yes, he was great with players, he got them, he liked them, he speaks their language, and yes, he was very apt at spotting players, buying on the cheap, and selling on for good money, but that's life at clubs like Bournemouth, Portsmouth and even West Ham.

But also, his knowledge of the game is unsurpassed, and his ability to change the course of a football match is ridiculously underrated. I have seen him, in dressing rooms at half-time, make tweaks, small or large changes to a team, and so often they have diverted the course of a game. It's the same on the training ground, getting the right people in around him, and helping players improve.

If a footballer like Paul Merson, when asked who is the best coach he ever worked with, says Harry Redknapp, then you have to take notice. Merse worked with George Graham, Arsène Wenger and Glenn Hoddle, to name just a few.

When the West Ham assistant manager job came up, I remember being at my parents', I had been at Liverpool a year, and Billy Bonds the manager at Upton Park was on the phone asking Dad to join him. What I remember was Dad mulling over the idea. It wasn't taken as some big chance, or his pathway into the big time. As I say, Dad isn't one for planning. Each day as it comes. Organised chaos.

So he was left mulling over Billy's offer, still very content at Bournemouth, *his* club, and all the security that came with that, and unsure whether taking a new role, especially that of assistant, was for him. In the end, I think it was the fact that Brian Tiler had been killed, two years earlier in the car crash in Rome, that might have influenced the decision to leave in 1992. Brian was his confidant at Bournemouth, his mate, his mentor, and without him things had changed a bit. Also, being an assistant was a way of learning about life at a bigger club without being in the line of fire.

Dad worked hard behind the scenes. He noticed that the youth set-up at the club was lost, and for a man who worked under Ron Greenwood that wouldn't do. Dad helped change all that, he got Jimmy Hampson in from Charlton, a West Ham fan, a great scout and youth development man, and in time the best talent in the south-east and beyond found its way to the club.

When Dad took the manager's job there in 1994, that interest in the kids never waned. In fact, it intensified. The thing about Dad is he cares. He really cares. I have heard so many stories about top managers: the youth team will be playing a game outside their office and they pull the curtains. Dad was always so into getting youth through the ranks and into the first team.

'We've got some good young players here' was a line that always greeted me over the phone on the day or the week he went to a new club, because it was the first thing he looked at. At West Ham, Dad always, if the first team weren't keeping him busy, went to see the youth games, got to know the youngsters, assured the youngsters that he liked them, that he wanted to know them and, with that, they felt confident that with hard work, they would get their chance in his first team.

Managers today lack that, they don't realise just how important their input and their interest in the young players can be to a youth team. By simply turning up and watching them train, that session's productivity would go up tenfold, but nowadays, perhaps slightly paralysed with the immediacy of the job and the fear of being sacked, academies are left to their own devices.

Under Dad, the club developed and was able to pick the likes of Rio, Frank Lampard, Joe Cole and Michael Carrick, but he would have loved combining them with maverick pros who could teach them something and excite the crowd. Paolo Di Canio was perfect. Dad was brave enough (or crazy enough, depending how you look at it) to go and get the Italian after he had pushed over the ref at Sheffield Wednesday in that infamous game against Arsenal in 1998, and was vilified by most for doing so. Not only did he get him, but Dad put him among young players and let them shine together. Brave, mad, genius.

All those attributes made Dad the boss he was, and he did great at West Ham, getting them up the league, winning the Intertoto Cup in 1999, playing the kind of football West Ham fans want to see. There was, however, that rascal gene in him, that temper that might boil like a kettle until he says maybe too much to the wrong person. Fallouts did happen, especially with those at board level. It's part of Dad; as I've said, we never saw it at home, but he will take so much and then his true feelings can spill out, arguments will be had, and in football jobs can be lost. That's what happened at West Ham in 2001, but it wouldn't be long before he got another job, this time back in the second tier, with Portsmouth.

He started there as director of football but, with time, that would never do, not for a man who loves the everyday nature of the job, being around the players, the staff and, once or twice a week, prowling the touchline with a match unfolding in front of him.

I always found it weird and tough to play against him and his teams. Knowing that my old man was sitting in the opposing dugout, both of us trying to ruin the other's day. I won't lie, I never felt comfortable with it.

At Liverpool, our manager Roy Evans could see it, and at times would come to me and say, 'Jamie, I know you don't enjoy this. Why don't you sit on the bench?' I never didn't want to play and would argue against that idea but, with hindsight, Roy knew and he was probably right. I never played well against West Ham. I found it hard. I would never not play well on purpose, but free-kicks I'm taking suddenly go thirty yards over the bar and I'm left thinking, that's weird. Roy was right, I was never myself. We usually beat them, don't get me wrong, but I never enjoyed it.

They were strange occasions. I am playing against my cousin, Frank, we're kicking each other, my uncle Frank is on the bench as assistant manager and my dad is the boss, trying to plot a win against my team. It was all a bit incestuous.

At Portsmouth, he rediscovered his mojo. I was slightly concerned that, after West Ham, he might struggle to find the right club, to be a success again, but that's Dad: he goes to Portsmouth, makes some very shrewd signings, gets the likes of Paul Merson in, wins promotion to the Premier League, and is back in the big time.

I think his success at Portsmouth was really his big moment. He had Jim Smith alongside him, a great character. Talking of characters, the club owner Milan Mandarić was larger than life, and it was inevitable that as well as they got on at times, there would be that clash, and that's exactly what happened and so Dad moves to the neighbours and rivals Southampton in 2004. That is what I mean when I say Dad's career and take on life can be organised chaos. Who else would have gone from Pompey to Southampton – teams whose supporters absolutely detest each other – and then head back to Portsmouth after? Chaos.

Despite the oddity of Dad's decision, I went down to play half a season with him at Southampton, and it was almost perfect. My knee was hanging on by a thread – that 2004–5 season would be my last dance as a professional footballer – and I went to try and help Dad and the club stay up. I needed cortisone injections and it probably wasn't the best idea playing, and I certainly wouldn't have done it for any other manager, but there was a chance of keeping them up, I liked Southampton as a club, still do, and we did our best there.

We almost did it. We had some good players, young and old, Peter Crouch, Rory Delap, David Higginbotham – good pros – but we narrowly missed out; results went against us, we gave up winning positions, and heartbreakingly we were relegated on the last day of the season.

One great result came against my old team, Liverpool, who we beat 2–0 at St Mary's in January 2005. I was in midfield up against Steven Gerrard and Didi Hamann, two old teammates, old pals, and very much among the best around. It was a classic Dad performance, his side full of energy and nous, and it was special to celebrate with him that night.

It was to be among my last moments as a footballer, and it felt fitting to end everything with the manager I'd started out with. The manager who just happened to be my dad. From now, though, I would be at football matches as a pundit. For a while, I covered Dad's games but it wasn't long before I felt that my relationship was making me lose my focus (perhaps like the days when I played against his teams).

I remember a game against Liverpool in December 2012. Dad was managing QPR and Luis Suárez was destroying them. They got beat heavily, and I said to camera that there was nothing wrong with QPR's tactics. I mean, they had been taken apart, and my assessment was clouded by our relationship. I soon asked the guys at Sky to be taken off Harry Redknapp matches.

But from afar, I could watch him, and as his biggest fan no one was prouder to see him lift the FA Cup in 2008, during his second spell at Portsmouth with a team full of big names, maybe coming to the end of their careers but enjoying playing in the fun atmosphere that Dad had created. I'd say it was like Bournemouth in the early days in terms of culture, but it was done with footballers who had played for the likes of Arsenal and Ajax, and others who would go on to play for the likes of Liverpool and Real Madrid.

The move to Tottenham later that year was a massive moment. Again, there was no big jump at the chance. In fact, he turned them down a year or so before. He was happy at Portsmouth, but I think he knew maybe he had taken them as far as he could. Tottenham rang him again and rushed him into a decision. We spoke and agreed that he should go and talk to them. My advice was that this was his big chance to really show his star quality at (and no offence to the other clubs) a really big football club.

He did just that. Immediately. He got in there, turned their bad form around, but then went on to reshape the team, identifying the talent they had there and, by simply playing them in their right positions, got the very best from them. Gareth Bale, Dad saw straight away his talent and got him flying with a bit of tough love, and Luka Modrić, a fantastic footballer, too often played in wide areas, but was someone who Dad knew had to be in the middle of the pitch where he was different class.

He proved so many people wrong at Spurs. He trusts himself, he knows his knowledge is there, and if someone says, 'Sorry, not possible,' he is driven to prove them wrong. Seeing him get Tottenham into the Champions League and win the Manager of the Season award in 2010 was a family highlight, and I could not have been prouder.

The club was a great fit, he enjoyed the football they played, he loved building a team, getting Peter Crouch and Jermaine Defoe back involved with him, European nights at White Hart Lane, it was all there, and I could tell, above all, that Dad was working with a big smile on his face.

Harder times followed at QPR from 2012, bad timing for everyone, and not a happy spell, but I can only look back on my old man's time in football with a combination of family pride and footballing respect.

Just before he went to QPR, there was talk about the England job, and of course I think he should have got it. I remember being in a car with Dad, coming home from a game. We had heard that the FA liked Dad for the job. Fabio Capello's tricky tenure ended in February 2012, and the public and the authorities wanted an Englishman. In the car, over the radio, we heard that Roy Hodgson had been appointed and, as good as a coach as Roy was, Dad and I were shocked. He had been doing a great job with Tottenham, and was many people's favourite for the role.

I know Dad was saddened by the decision, that he would have loved to manage his country, and thought about his own father, Pops, and the pride he would have had in the boy who he used to take to football matches after the war.

It wasn't to be, but while I was sad for him, both as a son and as someone who knows the game, I had seen the pressures that come with playing for England, let alone managing them, and I have to admit that there was some relief. I knew the kind of scrutiny Dad, and my mum, would have been under, how the lives of England managers are spun upside down by the newspapers and their clamour for news. It's a fine line between getting a knighthood and being sent to the Tower of London, and maybe, just maybe, I was glad it was a line my dad didn't have to walk.

Do I think he would have done a great job? I know he would have. He would have got players playing in the right positions, he would not have been fazed by the big egos he was working with and possibly having to drop, and he would have given the job and the team that sense of fun and energy that he gave most roles.

When it comes to those roles, Dad is a man of many. At home, he's simply the assistant manager to my mum, but in my career I have called him boss, I have gone into footballing battles for him, but I have also tried to beat his teams, he has tried to beat mine and I have watched from afar as he has pitted his wits against the very best and so often won. Today, I watch him play the game with my boys, and I will always think of him as my best mate. Yes, he has taken on many roles but his greatest is that of being my dad.

Over to you, son . . .

JAMIE

I love being at the match. I can get my fix on many levels. My work takes me to the Premier League, the elite, where I watch some of the best players, generational talents who each week are thrilling fans in every corner of the world. Watching one of my sons play sends me to academy games, where I see the lads striving, working hard, a collection of young men doing everything they can to make a dream come true. Then I have my grassroots stuff. My youngest boy, a toddler, who wants nothing more than to kick a ball around the garden and score a goal. You can't get more grassroots than that, can you?

I count myself very lucky with the work that I do with Sky. The game continues to flourish, the quality of player and manager continue to light up the Premier League, and while the past generations will all have their favourites from years gone by, the standard of footballer that we are fortunate enough to have in the domestic game can make the mind boggle.

Not that there aren't concerns. We love the game and, like anything we cherish, we hope it stays safe and comes to no harm. As a pundit, we have to spend too long talking about officials and law changes. VAR is a constant stick to beat the modern game with but it's here to stay and it needs to be perfected. The experience of the match-going football fan must be protected and then there are the players themselves.

We are seeing brilliantly coached young footballers; the facilities that they play within are incredible; and there is no doubt that academy football is producing technical footballers in numbers we've not seen before. There must be concerns, though, about helping young players be themselves. We have to ensure that some emerge who contrast from the pack. Those who dare to be different are what makes the game beautiful, but are young kids really being encouraged to try something not found in the coaching manuals? I'm not sure they are.

When I was playing, I knew my game. Get on the ball and keep possession. Get the team ticking over. Nothing too showy, I appreciate that, but what I knew from a young age was I had the ability to find the player who might flip a game on its head. So that's what I tried to do. Receive the ball, look up, thread a pass. Gazza, Steve McManaman, Robbie Fowler – there you go, weave your magic.

As I say, I watch one of my boys play at academy level and I'm both proud and excited to see him and his mates learning about the game. I can only guide him from the sidelines. He has the bug, which he caught so easily from our highly contagious family, but now, he'll learn a lot on his own not just about how playing the game can be the most beautiful thing in the world, but also that it has sharp teeth and, given the chance, it will bare them and bite him. I certainly have a few scars left.

As for those grassroots, that is simple for me right now. Out early in the morning, in our garden kicking a ball with my toddler. I can't remember a time as a boy when I didn't have a football at my feet, I can't remember a time when my brother and I weren't flinging open the back door and running around a small lawn, trying to impress Dad with a version of the latest goal we've seen on telly.

And so it goes on. My toddler, the ball up to his knees, dribbles across the garden, looks up and the ball is smashed into a pop-up goal. I can smile, and I can look forward to a future of chats about a shared devotion to the game with him. I can also dream. He has the sweetest left foot. I reckon he has a chance . . .

HARRY

You might find me on the golf course a bit more, you might find me watching the horses, but after six decades working in the game, I'm probably due a bit of a break. Not that I can stay away long. I love to be with Sandra, I love to have the grandkids round, a nice dinner out, the odd holiday, life is good, but whatever we all do together, my mind sways back to football. It always has and it always will.

Like Jamie, I have worries about the state of the game. I worry about the youth, and kids like my grandson in academy football that, compared to my day playing and managing, seems a world away from the senior stuff. I was spoiled and have explained in these pages about managers such as Ron Greenwood who made the kids a priority. The fact that, today, many of the academies aren't even in the same postcode as the first-team training complexes tells you everything, and I can only hope that football clubs and managers in the future work on finding a reconnect.

I still sit back, and watch a match. Seeing footballers has always give me such a buzz. I can look back on that day I watched Duncan Edwards, that mountain of a young man, run out at Highbury in 1958 and be in awe again. I can smile at managing Paolo Di Canio, two men from very different cultures, but somehow we made it work. And now I can sit and watch a talent like Jude Bellingham, who might just push the country on to some long overdue success.

I have always loved the players. When everything is said and done, it's all about them. We can coach them, direct them; pundits can dissect systems and new ways of doing things; but it is the players, their efforts, that make the game special.

So what of the future? Well, tactics come and go, and so do tacticians. There have been plenty of great footballing teams to drool over recently; and football being played from the back in tidy patterns of play might have me pulling my hair out (especially when done by players simply not good enough to), but that won't last. We'll have to wait to see what's around the corner. What the new fad will be. Personally I hope it's flying wingers and a big centre-forward. You never know, they could catch on?

What is certain is the gratitude I have for a game that has given me and my family everything. It has offered me experiences, friendships and a way of life that nothing else could have. Yes, there are big moments, cup finals, full stadiums and great players, but what I love to do is to reminisce about the small but fantastic things.

A day out with my dad. Going to the match. The bus, the crowd, a walk, a flask of tea, and meeting a bloke from Bolton or Manchester or Birmingham, and talking about our teams. It felt exotic. Making my way in the game and that sense of discovery never stopped. Through football, I have learned about new cultures, and new beliefs, in ways that a boy born in post-war Poplar would otherwise never have dreamed of.

I can share all of that now with my grandkids. When news broke that Liverpool's great, old captain Ron Yeats had died recently, some of the family were together, sharing some fish and chips. My son Mark showed us a lovely photo of him, Jamie and a few of the Liverpool boys enjoying a dinner with Ron some years ago. My grandson asked who that was. I told him that the man in the photo was a great old centre-half. His eyes lit up. 'We could play a bit in my day,' I told him. He might just have believed me.

Now, when the phone goes and I can see it is one of my boys, nothing changes. It is how it's always been:

'Did you see the match?'

Of course I bloody did.

Acknowledgements

A huge thank you from us both to everyone at Little, Brown for their work, expertise and support in making this book. Kirsteen Astor, Holly Blood, Andreas Campomar, Alex Cooper, Aimee Kitson, Linda Silverman and Howard Watson; you have made this experience truly a family affair.

Thanks to Nicky Johnston and his team for their fantastic cover photography.

To Richard, Sara and Madison at M&C Saatchi Merlin for all that you do.

Thank you to Nick Walters at David Luxton Associates for all his great work.

Thanks to Mark. The best son and brother anyone could have.

And finally to Leo Moynihan who wrote this book with us. Thank you for getting us together and all your hard work. It's been a pleasure.